"**B**uckle up for an enlightening journey! Heather Crider masterfully guides readers through a profound exploration of self-discovery, weaving in powerful stories, illustrative examples, and a comprehensive framework for conquering any obstacle life throws our way. This book is an essential read for anyone striving to become their best self while navigating the complexities of the business world. Unlike quick-fix guides, this book encourages deep reflection and deliberate practice of its strategies, making it worth taking the time to absorb and implement. Crider adeptly addresses the pervasive issue of imposter syndrome, breaking down the neuroscience and offering practical strategies to help us surmount life's challenges."

—Noelle Robinson, Founder of The Sound Spa, Certified Sound Therapist, and Health and Wellness Advocate.

"My first concern was how a neuroscience book could be practical, useful, and not boring. *Believe In Yourself More Than Your Grandma* by Heather Crider put my concerns to rest. She shared stories that were profoundly vulnerable, impactful, and relevant. This book was packed full of frameworks that anyone at any level can immediately use to achieve significant growth and results. It's a great book with great stories and even better tools."

—John Barada, ChFC, RFC, CCPS, President College Planning Consultants, LLC

"Wow, as someone who has studied many of the principles described in this book, Heather Crider has done a superb job of translating what would be perceived as complex neuroscience into bite-sized, digestible pieces. How she explained through her own stories and weaved in neuroscience is incredibly useful for anyone from a budding solopreneur to an accomplished leader. She addresses many common issues high achievers face, including imposter syndrome, stress, guilt, procrastination, and productivity. I highly recommend this book for anyone wishing to get more out of their life while overcoming their inner struggles, once and for all!"

—Tessa Greenspan, Author, From Outhouse to Penthouse

"This book is a great combination of science and real-world stories that illustrate a simple approach! As a woman who has spent my career in a male-dominated industry, I lived a long time in the world of imposter syndrome/fake it till you make it—this definitely resonated a ton. It's a great book with lots of takeaways. Thank you so much for sharing it with the world."

—Kristin Tucker, Co-Founder and Managing Principal of TDK Technologies, LLC.

Believe In Yourself More Than Your Grandma

Unleash Your Superpower Through Simple Neuroscience

Heather J. Crider

Believe In Yourself More Than Your Grandma: Unleash Your Superpower Through Simple Neuroscience

Copyright ©2024 by Heather J. Crider

IBSN 979-8-218-97468-8

For more information, hello@heatherjcrider.com

Empire Wealth International Publishing

Author Photo by Erica White

Contents

Foreword

In a world brimming with self-help books and quick-fix solutions, "Believe In Yourself – More than Your Grandma" by Heather J. Crider stands out as a beacon of authenticity and transformative power. This isn't just another motivational read; it's a journey into the very core of what makes us human, guided by a true Neuroscience Yoda.

As you open these pages, prepare to embark on an odyssey of self-discovery that will challenge your perceptions, reframe your beliefs, and ultimately unleash your inner superpower. Heather doesn't just tell you to believe in yourself; she shows you how, step by step, neuron by neuron.

Drawing from her deeply personal experiences, Heather lays bare the struggles and triumphs that have shaped her path. With raw honesty, she invites you to confront your own "gremlins"—those insidious thoughts and beliefs that have taken root in the fertile soil of your mind. But fear not, for in exposing these shadows, she also illuminates the way forward.

I love the fact that this is a simplified tome. Heather has a unique ability to blend cutting-edge neuroscience with heartfelt wisdom. Like a skilled alchemist, she transforms complex concepts into accessible tools, empowering you to rewire your brain and rewrite your story. You'll learn to observe your thought patterns in what some may call "non-anxious awareness," a superpower that allows you to stand firm in the face of change and uncertainty.

As you progress through the chapters, you'll find yourself equipped with a veritable utility belt of possibility. Weekly challenges push you beyond your comfort zone, while the actionable toolbox provides practical strategies for implementing lasting change. The daily habits Heather introduces are not mere routines but rituals for cultivating sustained well-being and unlocking your full potential.

She doesn't preach from a pedestal of perfection; instead, she sits beside you on the park bench of life, acknowledging our shared humanity in all its beautiful imperfections. Her words resonate with a simple yet profound truth: you matter, and the world needs your unique gifts now more than ever.

As you delve into these pages, you'll discover that she has achieved something remarkable. She has distilled the essence of personal growth and neuroscientific insight into a "vitamin for your mind and soul" – a daily dose of empowerment that nourishes your spirit and expands your horizons.

So, dear reader, as you stand on the precipice of change, know that you hold in your hands more than just a book. You hold a compass, a map, and a trusted guide for the journey ahead. Let Heather J. Crider be your Neuroscience Yoda, believing in you even as you learn to believe in yourself.

Open your mind, open your heart, and prepare to unlock the superpower that has been within you all along. The adventure begins now, and the possibilities are limitless. Welcome to "Believe in Yourself" – your transformative journey awaits.

Simon T. Bailey, Brilliance Researcher, Innovator, and Award-Winning Keynote Speaker

Preface

What's the connection between tales of grandmothers and beliefs and, say, your life, your team, or your business? Stick with me for a bit, and I'll explain why this book isn't just another to collect dust on your bookshelf.

Flashback years ago to the day I stepped into the world of business ownership, buying my first business, a financial agency. There I was, at my first regional advisor meeting, feeling out of my depth and intimidated. Despite my years navigating the complexity and unpredictability of the corporate seas, this was different. Now, everything hinged on the insights I could glean from such gatherings—no cushy corporate lifelines or safety nets, just me, my decisions, and their consequences. My livelihood and success of my business, and my future, now rested on how well I could navigate and act upon meetings such as this. Thrilling, yet terrifying as hell!

As the meeting droned on, each presentation blending into the next, my attention wavered. Representatives from various companies made their pitches, all claiming superiority but none breaking the monotony. I remember becoming glassy-eyed and bored, my thoughts drifting despite myself. The room, with its orderly rows of chairs facing the presentation easel and the coffee table to the side, offered little distraction from the monotony. However, the window's view of downtown St. Louis offered a brief respite—at least I had this view to occupy my attention. Little did I know, something—or someone—was about to disrupt the monotony.

Then, the next presenter, Rob, took the stage. Despite wearing the same standard-issue gray or blue suit as the others, complete with the company-logoed lapel pin, something about him immediately caught my attention. As he walked to the front, I sat up straighter, tilting my head, ready to listen more intently than I had all day.

"Hi, my name is Rob, and I'm thrilled to be here with you fine folks today," he began, sharing glimpses into his life that resonated with me. He talked about his small-town roots, not far from where my journey began, his days playing college and minor league baseball—a detail that stuck with me as a fellow baseball enthusiast—and his recent marriage. This was his first time meeting any of us, yet he spoke as if addressing old friends.

What Rob shared about his company wasn't revolutionary. His products were similar to what we'd already seen. However, he still held my attention. He presented with absolute conviction and belief. *How* he shared made all the difference. It wasn't just a sales pitch; it was a belief—a deep, unwavering belief. This wasn't about dazzling us with jargon or pushing products. Rob was all about genuine connection, belief in his work, and the conviction that he could make a difference. Now that I recall this moment, I realize meeting Rob was instrumental for me then and transformed how I viewed my career and my approach to my clients. He wasn't just selling; he was believing.

And it was infectious.

I had witnessed plenty of sales presentations with amazing products and the presenter cramming them down your throat. What Rob did was different because he believed in who he was. Not arrogance or cockiness. I even discussed his belief with my manager, John, and remember asking his opinion. John replied, "When people believe in themselves and what they're doing, they're confident, not arrogant. And to be effective with anyone, you must believe in yourself first." Great advice, John!

Rob's belief in his work, products, and, importantly, in us, was a game-changer. I dove deep into learning everything I could about his offerings, integrating them into my business in ways that genuinely benefited my clients. Our collaboration over the years was fruitful, and at one point, during another regional meeting, Rob even stood up and mentioned how grateful he was for having met me. I was grateful to have met him, too. But more importantly, he opened my eyes to how I viewed myself in these situations and how I felt about my own beliefs.

Seeking an understanding of success has become an obsession for me: the idea that the secret sauce to success boils down to believing in yourself.

It sounds straightforward, doesn't it? Yet, diving deep into the stories of those who've soared and those who've stumbled reveals a strikingly simple truth. The people who believed in themselves had happier lives, larger bank accounts, and more social networks and displayed a higher sense of overall fulfillment and purpose. Simply whether they believed they could or not.

If belief were so simple and a significant factor in success, why are so many people struggling to achieve the performance they desire, still trying to crack the success code?

Here's my take: It's one thing to say you believe in yourself, but it's another to let that belief shape how you see yourself, the decisions you make, and the habits you form. That's where the magic happens.

Our self-perception and the beliefs we hold about our capabilities play a pivotal role in shaping our lives. Our experiences and environments often influence this intricate dance between perception and belief. Yet, amidst this complexity, it remains within our power to choose which beliefs we allow to guide us. Our brains are hard-wired to focus on negativity as a survival mechanism, and acknowledging this can empower us to shift our focus towards more positive and empowering beliefs.

How we learn how to view ourselves and the world around us and how we process and manage our feelings about ourselves and the world around us all matter. Our brains evolve naturally and essentially the same. However, we all have different thoughts, feelings, beliefs and viewpoints. Our environments, influences, and experiences contribute to how we view ourselves, thus leading to our habits and behaviors and how we respond to how we think. You could argue that the way we think is what really matters, and you wouldn't be wrong. But the deeply embedded viewpoint you have about yourself is the driving force in every recognizable conscious thought as well as the background subconscious thoughts that control our emotions and behaviors.

There is an overwhelming amount of influence we are exposed to during our life that shape our thoughts and our beliefs. Many people are exposed to the exact circumstances yet believe and behave differently. Why is this? The difference lies in how an individual feels about themselves and what they choose believe is possible.

Take Arnold Schawrznager, for example. Starting as the youngest Austrian to win Mr. Olympia, who, driven by a childhood fascination with American movies, transitioned into acting through sheer belief and determination. Despite initial challenges with language and acting skills, his relentless pursuit of opportunities and breakthrough roles in films as an action actor propelled him to international stardom. He believed in his ability to make audiences laugh and actively sought comedic roles, but was met with resistance. How could a bodybuilder with a funny accent be funny? But this did not stop him. His self-belief drove him to put himself in unfamiliar territory and a financial risk. Arnold's belief in his ability led to him pitching an epic move for the movie "Twins." The studio believed it was a significant risk and not commercially viable for Arnold to play such a comedic role. Schwarzenegger, however, was determined to land the role. He believed in the movie's potential and his ability to make it successful. He made a bold proposal to demonstrate his commitment and belief in the project and agreed to forgo his upfront salary in exchange for a percentage of the film's profits. This meant he would only receive a guaranteed income if the movie were successful.

The gamble paid off. "Twins" became a box office success, grossing over $216 million worldwide. Schwarzenegger's belief in himself and the movie earned him a significantly higher pay-out than his usual salary due to the profit-sharing agreement.

So, like Arnold, you can believe big, or you can believe small. Either way, the power of belief can profoundly affect the outcomes in your life.

Arnold Schwarzenegger's journey embodies the transformative power of belief. It became a testament to his commitment to challenging himself and pursuing his artistic vision, even when faced with initial doubt, all starting with the power of belief. Yet, this begs the question: If belief is so powerful, why do many still struggle to reach their desired levels of success?

There is a universal truth: those who harbor a deep, unshakeable belief in their potential often transcend obstacles and achieve greatness. It's one thing to say you believe in yourself; it's another entirely to let that belief deeply influence your actions and perspective. This is where the magic happens.

The ABCs of Reflection—Awareness, Beliefs, and Choices—serve as a guiding framework to navigate this journey. By becoming acutely aware of our beliefs, challenging those that limit us, and choosing to adopt empowering beliefs, we set the stage for profound personal transformation. Whether aiming to overcome a habit, achieve professional success, or enhance personal relationships, the beliefs we nurture and act upon determine our path and its outcomes.

Belief can pay off in our lives financially, in relationships, in experiences, and in many other ways.

Anything you choose to believe is possible. If you want to quit smoking and believe hypnosis can help you, then it is likely to be more effective. If you believe you are destined for greatness, you have a higher percentage of achieving greatness. If you believe you are a failure. You are more likely to display behavior that reinforces this belief. If you have doubts about the effectiveness of a treatment or a process, the overall result will likely not be suitable for your goals. If you believe you will fail at your marriage your behavior will reinforce this belief. If you believe that you can improve your marriage or be a better mate, you will seek more positive communication strategies or ways to improve yourself.

As you delve into this book, I invite you to explore the power of belief with an open mind and heart and engage with the concept of belief as a superpower. Let these pages' stories, neuroscience-backed principles, and strategies guide you toward a more empowered, belief-driven life.

Remember, at the core of every success story is a simple yet profound conviction: belief in oneself. It's that simple—and that transformative.

Introduction

"It's your power. Take It Back."

I t's Your Power, Take It Back. What does this statement evoke within you? Have you identified your superpower, be it an innate talent, a learned skill, or a particular mindset that sets you apart? Pause momentarily and define your super-power. Or, if it eludes you, what you dream it could be. Write it down.

Imagine living each day infused with this unique strength. Picture the fulfillment, the ease in overcoming stress, the surge in productivity, and the ripple of kindness and prosperity stemming from you. Such is the power of living aligned with your superpower.

As a child, I loved superheroes. My fascination with su-perheroes wasn't just about the allure of flying or the fantasy of wielding a lasso of truth. It was the deeper yearning to be invincible enough to navigate challenges, assist others, and maneuver through life with unmatched precision and confi-dence. This childhood dream, however, seemed to fade against the backdrop of life's complexities, fading into the monochromatic shades of fear, uncertainty, and doubt.

Reclaiming my superpowers as an adult has been a journey back to myself, a renaissance of the belief that the power I sought externally had been within me all along.

This revelation crystallized further when life presented me with challenges in my personal and professional life.

When my son was just a baby, he faced what were technically minor health challenges, but at the time, they felt anything but minor to me. As my second child—and my first boy—he introduced me to a new level of parenting stress. I found myself navigating truly unfamiliar waters. Around the same time, I ran my wealth management firm, which was going well. Then, out of the blue, I was invited to speak at a conference for professional women about finances. Doubts swirled within me, and the timing felt off. I was worried about leaving my son, even more so because I wasn't sure I was the right person to be advising these accomplished women.

So, I did what I always do when I'm stuck—I called my grandmother, the matriarch whose advice was always a blend of hard truths and unconditional support, regardless of whether I felt prepared to face it. I told her about the conference and how I felt—nervous, unsure, and doubting if I should go.

"I'm nervous. I don't think I can go," I confessed to her.

"And why not?" she probed, cutting through my surface-level concerns to the heart of the matter.

"I'm not experienced enough, nor do I feel qualified enough to offer the advice they seek."

"What's this really about, Heather Jo?" she pressed, always knowing how to peel back the layers of my excuses.

"My inexperience in speaking to such a large, professional audience terrifies me. What if they see me as a fraud?"

Her response, delivered with her characteristic charm and wisdom, was exactly what I needed to hear.

"They invited you, which means they see value in what you can offer. You're more than capable, and your heart's in the right place. This opportunity is tailor-made for you, and I believe in you. Now, it's time for you to start believing in yourself."

She was spot on. I can still vividly recall that moment, sitting in my car outside my office, the sunlight casting a warm glow over me as I grappled with the decision before me. Opting to leave my son for just a day was a daunting thought, but the real battle was with the shadows of self-doubt that loomed over me. In that instance, I leaned on my grandmother's unwavering belief in me and took the stage a few days later, addressing 250 women. It was the most significant presentation of my career to date. I was fully present, delivering my message with all the knowledge and heart I possessed. I walked away with a sense of pride for having shown up and being myself in front of that crowd.

Yet, no sooner had I stepped off the stage than the familiar cloud of self-doubt crept back in. The what-ifs began to haunt me. What if my message didn't resonate? What if my fears of inadequacy were evident? The self-doubt was relentless, a thick fog that threatened to obscure my sense of achievement. Fortunately, or perhaps ironically, the immediate demands of caring for my son upon my return home provided a welcome distraction from the mire of my insecurities.

Yet, the battle with self-doubt didn't end there; it's an ongoing journey between confidence and questioning. This recurring dance with self-doubt, a familiar barrier to joy, has often prevented me from fully engaging with life's peaks and valleys. My grandmother, a beacon of hope and unwavering belief possessed an uncanny ability to see the potential in me, even when I was oblivious to it. Her passing left a profound void, yet it sparked a crucial realization: the belief I had borrowed from her needed to become deeply rooted within me.

Her wisdom, delivered with a unique mix of sass and kindness, sometimes stern yet always supportive, has guided me throughout my life. It inspired the creation of my podcast, "Go Reflect Yourself," which continues her legacy, challenging us to introspect and hold ourselves accountable in our quest for personal growth.

My grandmother's belief in me, a constant source of strength, underscored a vital lesson: the belief we seek from others must ultimately be found within ourselves.

This book is an homage to that transformation, a guide crafted to inspire you to unearth and harness your superpower. It's a narrative that weaves together personal anecdotes, the science of self-belief, and practical strategies designed to elevate your journey toward self-assurance, leadership excellence, and a life that resonates with extraordinary potential.

More than a personal quest, this journey of self-belief is pivotal in cultivating a culture of confidence within teams and organizations. By embracing your superpower, you not only elevate yourself but also become a pillar of support and belief for those around you, fostering an environment ripe for success and cohesion.

I aim to ignite a belief in you that transcends even the most steadfast external support, even that belief a grandmother could have in you. To reveal the superpower you seek is already within you, ready to be unleashed. This guide invites you to not only dream of greatness but to actively pursue it, inspiring a ripple effect of belief and excellence in every aspect of your life and beyond.

"It's Your Power, Take It Back"

Throughout this book, you'll explore the story of my journey from feeling perpetually out of place and deeply insecure, as if marked by an invisible scarlet letter, to discovering the foundation of true confidence. This quest revealed a profound truth: with each achievement, each venture into the unknown, and each risk, I was not only building my confidence but also stepping into a realm of empowerment I had never imagined possible. The paradox was striking—the moments I felt most stripped of power and confidence were directly tied to my failures in honoring my own promises.

The transformation was most profound when I embraced radical responsibility, a principle that became my beacon of empowerment. This journey highlighted the essential role of radical responsibility and self-integrity in achieving personal growth and fulfillment. Embracing this path requires honesty, compassion, and openness, not just for personal enlightenment but as a beacon for those we lead.

As leaders, we bear a unique responsibility not only to pursue our empowerment but also to foster an environment where others are encouraged to reclaim their power. By embodying radical responsibility, we set a precedent, teaching by example that the most profound empowerment comes from within. We inspire those around us to recognize and harness their inherent strength, guiding them toward their own journeys of self-discovery and fulfillment.

So, as you navigate through the pages ahead, let this book serve as a reminder to both reclaim your power and illuminate the path for others. Remember, true leadership is not just about leading with confidence—it's about empowering others to find their confidence and strength. "It's Your Power, Take It Back" is more than a personal mantra; it's a call to action for every leader to inspire and uplift, turning individual empowerment into a collective resurgence of strength and purpose.

Chapter One

In the Silence of Doubt: Origin of Belief

"Your chances of success in any undertaking can always be measured by your belief in yourself." Robert Collier

At the heart of every achievement lies a belief—a conviction that, regardless of its origin, generates undeniable energy. But have you ever paused to ponder the essence of belief? Let's delve into the origins of belief, its nature, and the processes behind its formation. What shapes our beliefs about ourselves and the world around us?

Have you ever thought deeply about the origin of belief, what a belief actually is, why you believe what you do, or how a belief is formed?

Simplistically, a belief is a perspective that you choose to perceive as true. But why? Where does it come from? How does the brain process it? How do you get a thought? How do you choose a belief? Why do you believe what you do about yourself or others?

Belief Formation

Beliefs are formed through various factors, including personal experiences, cultural influences, education, and emotions. While some beliefs are based on objective evidence, others stem from more subjective interpretations or faith; this aligns with the notion of choosing a belief to hold true.

Neuroscience reveals that our inherently superstitious brains construct beliefs from vast amounts of information, distilling them into personal and ethical assumptions. This subjective process, shaped by individual experiences and biases, influences our perception of the world, meaning we choose our perspectives based on how our brains interpret sensory inputs. Groundbreaking research in neuroscience sheds light on the development of self-belief, the roots of doubts and fears, and how these elements affect our decisions, performance, and ability to learn. This fascinating journey into our minds reveals how we construct beliefs, balancing the quest for accuracy with the need for personally meaningful truths.

One aspect of this research shows that we construct our beliefs to fulfill two sometimes conflicting goals: forming accurate beliefs to inform our decisions and forming desirable beliefs that we value for their own sake. This suggests a complex interplay between the desire for accuracy and the desire for beliefs that support our self-concept and goals.

The Neuroscience of Belief

The neurophysiological mechanisms behind belief formation underscore the vital roles of specific brain regions in shaping our decisions and preferences. Brain areas like the prefrontal cortex, medial orbitofrontal cortex, insula, and cingulate are instrumental in mediating subjective preference judgments, which are crucial for belief development. This complex interplay between our emotional experiences and cognitive processes not only dictates our everyday decisions but also profoundly influences our learning and our capacity to tackle challenges. Understanding how the brain integrates past experiences, emotions, and subjective preferences, we gain valuable insights into the unconscious processes steering our decision-making, highlighting the intricate relationship between our neurological functions and beliefs.

Research also delves into how beliefs about intelligence, such as fixed versus growth mindsets, affect learning and response to feedback. Individuals with a growth mindset are far more likely to engage in processes that help them learn from errors. In contrast, those with a fixed mindset might focus more on self-critical rumination, affecting their ability to learn from mistakes. The distinction between a growth and a fixed mindset illustrates the profound effect of beliefs on our ability to learn from mistakes and evolve. Embracing a growth mindset fosters resilience and adaptability, which are crucial for overcoming life's hurdles.

Science offers insights into the objective phenomena of belief formation, yet it is our personal and subjective experiences that genuinely shape our reality. This dynamic interplay between measurable science and individual perception underscores the complexity of choosing our beliefs, guiding us toward understanding and navigating our perceptions to achieve happiness despite the inherent limitations of our brain's development. So, while science can provide insights into how we perceive and form beliefs, it can't definitively say whether or not we "choose" them.

Awareness

Belief, thought, and awareness are foundational in all we undertake, yet the natural maturation of our brains can obscure our happiness and introduce life's challenges.

Mark Waldman, a mentor whose insights have profoundly influenced me, highlights in his book "Neurowisdom: The New Brain Science of Money, Happiness, and Success,"[1] co-authored with Dr. Chris Manning, that self-awareness and social awareness are pivotal for achieving lifelong success. These elements, Waldman asserts, are the ultimate pillars of wealth, leading to happiness and fulfillment.

From birth, our journey toward awareness is both complex and evolving. Initially, our understanding and consciousness are limited as our brains are in the early stages of development. As we grow, particularly through childhood, we transition

---

1. Neurowisdom: The New Brain Science of Money, Happiness, and Success: https://www.amazon.com/NeuroWisdom-Brain-Science-Happiness-Success/dp/1682303055

from seeking basic needs to developing a more nuanced awareness of our desires and goals.

Children's simple declarations of "give me" or "I want" exemplify the early stages of goal-oriented behavior driven by instinct. Yet, they encounter frustration as they grow and learn from their environments. This frustration stems from the challenge of balancing their emerging self-awareness with society's expectations, a task made difficult by the incomplete development of crucial brain circuits responsible for self and social understanding.

The insula and anterior cingulate cortex, key regions governing self-awareness and empathy, which are part of the salience network, are not fully developed until well into our twenties or even early thirties. These circuits form the heart of the social brain, enabling emotional awareness and empathy towards others. This developmental delay can impact young adults' and teenagers' ability to navigate the complex intricacies of relationships and show genuine compassion, contributing to misunderstandings and conflicts. With the recent attention given to the salience network in the relationship of moral factors (e.g., moral emotions, moral reasoning) in the decision-making process, neuroscientists have begun to offer helpful frameworks for understanding the interplay between the brain, morality, and human decision-making. These studies link to high criminal activity and even high divorce rates among twenty-year-olds due to their rebellious nature and inability to process complex relationship dynamics emotionally.

The fundamental components of our human nature shape the landscape of our social lives. The various facets of empathy, including affective arousal/emotional sharing, empathic concern, and perspective-taking, have unique contributions as subcomponents of morality. This review helps us understand how primary forms of empathy, morality, and justice are substantialized in early development.[2] It provides valuable information to gain new insights into the underlying neurobiological precursors of the social brain, enabling future translation toward therapeutic and medical interventions.

Acknowledging awareness's significance in personal growth makes it clear that nurturing this skill is essential. Though wonderfully adaptable, our brains require conscious effort to strengthen areas like the insula and anterior cingulate cortex. You don't need to fully understand the brain or even remember any of the neuroscience data cited. The connection is simply to state how complex the brain is and that the brain's development affects behavior and decision-making and forms memories, which affect decision-making. Therefore, self-awareness is critical. Enhancing self-awareness not only aids in personal evolution but also enriches our interactions and relationships with others.

Nurturing our awareness unlocks the potential for significant personal and professional growth, setting a foundation for a fulfilling life. We can enhance our cognitive and emotional understanding through deliberate practice and reflection, paving the way for a journey marked by success and contentment.

---

2. Singer T. The neuronal basis of empathy and fairness. Novartis Found Symp. 2007;278:20-30; discussion 30-40, 89-96, 216-21. PMID: 17214308.

Mindfulness

Strengthening self-awareness is pivotal for personal evolution, success, and fulfillment. It involves becoming acutely aware of oneself as the focal point of attention. While many of us are adept at directing our attention inward, our capacity to comprehend or interpret this self-awareness, especially regarding our beliefs, often falls short.

Have you ever found yourself so lost in thought that you've overlooked your immediate actions or even the people around you? Whether it's running a red light while engrossed in your musings or tuning out a conversation to the extent of not recalling a single word—yes, so sorry, Sawyer (my now 16-year-old) I'm guilty of this more times than I'd like to admit. Or perhaps, have you ever spun a narrative so steeped in fear and doubt that it became your perceived reality?

Reflecting on the days when my children faced challenges at school, my immediate internal dialogue spiraled into self-criticism and catastrophic predictions.

"I'm a terrible mother," I'd think, "My children are doomed to fail, bound to quit school and live in my basement forever!"

This reaction was an automatic response rooted in fear, uncertainty, and doubt (FUD)—a vivid example of my brain's autopilot taking the helm, steering me into a storm of emotional turmoil without a second thought.

Imagine your brain as a highly efficient worker who knows when to conserve energy and when to go full throttle. Much like a seasoned pilot switching to autopilot mode during a routine flight, our brains operate in two primary modes: deliberate and automatic. In its deliberate mode, the brain is like a focused CEO, consciously making decisions, planning strategies, and solving complex problems. However, our brain prefers to work in the background, using its automatic mode—our mental autopilot. This mode handles the daily operations without the need for conscious thought, from driving to work to typing an email, relying on habits, reflexive reactions, and emotional responses that are ingrained through natural repetition.

The science behind this mental autopilot involves fascinating areas of our brain. The basal ganglia are pivotal in turning repeated actions into effortless habits, creating neural pathways that make future executions almost second nature. Meanwhile, the Default Mode Network (DMN) takes over when we're not focused on specific tasks, allowing our minds to wander, daydream, and process information without our active engagement. This autopilot mode is incredibly efficient, enabling us to save our mental energy for the big decisions and creative thinking that truly require our conscious attention.

Your Autopilot is Speaking on Your Behalf

There's a nuanced challenge with our mental autopilot. Similar to how an airplane's autopilot system is not designed for every phase of flight, our mental autopilot isn't ideal for every situation (as I described when dealing with my children or accidentally running a red light). Emotional intelligence teaches us that unchecked emotions can hijack our autopilot, leading to impulsive decisions or emotional reactions that may not serve us well; this is precisely where the power of awareness comes into play.

At its core, mindfulness is the practice of intensely focusing on our present thoughts and actions. Far from being just a modern buzzword, mindfulness is an essential tool for daily self-awareness, empowering us to manage our thoughts actively. This practice, deeply rooted in metacognition, involves recognizing and overseeing our cognitive processes. By engaging the prefrontal cortex—our mental command center—mindfulness boosts our ability to concentrate and effectively execute tasks, debunking misconceptions and highlighting its crucial role in enhancing our mental clarity and task performance.

The more attention you give and frame your awareness on doing something, the more chance your mind has to carry out that task, and the better you will be at focusing on accomplishing the task.

We can recognize when we are operating on autopilot and take back control by embracing mindfulness practices. This awareness ensures we're fully present, making conscious choices that matter. Mindfulness goes beyond noting our automated daily routines; it is a strategy for deciding when to engage actively, guiding us toward our goals in both personal and professional realms.

Understanding and managing our brain's autopilot mode reveals the depth of our day spent on cruise control and highlights moments needing our deliberate attention. Self-aware mindfulness establishes the optimal conditions for our brain to prioritize what truly matters, empowering us to scrutinize our beliefs and their origins. With mindfulness, we gain the clarity to question and understand our beliefs, the driving force behind our thoughts and actions. Without this awareness, our beliefs remain unexamined, subtly steering our life's direction from the shadows.

Chapter Summary:

There is a complex interplay between the desire for accuracy and the desire for beliefs that support our self-concept and goals. The journey exploring the Silence of Doubt delves into the intricate dance between doubt and fear and their profound effects on our identity and self-worth. Recognizing when our brain shifts into autopilot can be crucial in this exploration. Our automatic reactions are often rooted in deep-seated doubts and fears, influencing how we see ourselves and our capabilities. By beginning the journey of self-discovery and taking radical responsibility for our thoughts and actions, we embark on a path that allows us to confront these doubts directly.

Through reflective practices, we learn to pause and observe the autopilot in action, identifying the internal barriers that hold us back. This reflection is not about rigorous self-examination but rather about gently acknowledging where our automatic modes lead us astray from our true selves. It hints at the essence of mindfulness—enhancing our awareness of the present moment and our patterns of thought, emotion, and behavior. This process does not just spotlight the areas where autopilot serves us well; it illuminates the shadows cast by doubt and fear, offering insights into overcoming them.

By incorporating strategies for confronting doubt and fostering a deeper understanding of ourselves, we can uncover how these automatic responses impact our self-worth and identity. This chapter is not just an exploration of the mind's tendency to operate on autopilot; it's a guide to recognizing and dismantling the doubts and fears that fuel it, setting the stage for a journey of profound self-discovery and empowerment.

Go Reflect Yourself Reflection Exercise:
Awareness and Self-Examination

Awareness will set you free, and so will self-examination! At the end of each chapter, there will be a "Go Reflect Yourself" section. Have a special notebook handy where you can take your time and be free to write and answer as many or all of the reflection prompts as you desire.

You can also request the accompanying Go Reflect Yourself Journal to coincide with the reflection prompts in this book. To get your copy, email hello@heatherjcrider.com.

REFLECTION QUESTIONS:
- Are you open to growth, learning, and self-examination?

- How committed are you to your current beliefs?

- Reflect on the reasons behind your commitment or lack thereof?

- Identify your default beliefs about various aspects of life. Write down whatever comes to mind without judgment.

- Examine the nature of these beliefs. Are they positive or negative? Do they align with your goals and contribute to your desired reality?

- When your mind begins to wander, what triggers this wandering, and how do you usually respond?

- What Insights or takeaways came to you while reading this chapter?

For the next few days, practice mindfulness by simply ob-serving your thoughts as they arise. Greet them with a mental note: "Oh, hey, there you are! I noticed you." This act of noticing is essentially a mental exercise, strengthening your meta-awareness. You don't need to force a change or force anything; just noticing your awareness strengthens your ability to build awareness. So notice away!

Reflective Examples:

Example 1:

During an early phase of my career, at a company event, my boss approached me while I was with a friend. He extended his hand to my friend, saying, "Pleasure to meet you." In a moment of nervous autopilot, I blurted out, "Nice to meet you too," directly to my boss—who I had known and worked with daily for months. The moment the words left my mouth, a wave of embarrassment washed over me. My brain, caught in a whirlwind of anxiety, had momentarily shut down.

While driving home that evening, my mind replayed the incident on a loop. "How could I say something so foolish? He's going to think I'm not only absent-minded but outright incompetent," I thought, berating myself. My thoughts were not just about a slip of the tongue; they were a reflection of a deeper belief that had taken root within me—I was convinced of my own stupidity.

For days, maybe weeks, I carried this belief with me, letting it color my interactions and decision-making. It starkly illustrat-ed how a moment of unawareness and an autopilot response could spiral into a profoundly ingrained narrative about one's self-worth. At that time, I wasn't even conscious that these were just thoughts, not the truth. My awareness of my own thought process was virtually nonexistent; I felt stupid and accepted that feeling as reality.

Example 2:

During one of our sessions, James, a neuro performance coaching client, consistently countered my suggestions with a dismissive, "Yeah, if it were only that easy."

This pattern became so recurrent that I decided it was time for a direct approach.

In one of my famous coaching lines, I asked him, "May I respond and offer a suggestion?" He reluctantly said yes!

"James, I've noticed a pattern in your responses. Whenever I offer a suggestion or a solution, you deflect with skepticism. And respond often with "Yeah, if it were only that easy." "Have you observed this as well?"

Caught off-guard but intrigued, James admitted, "I guess you're right. I do say that a lot, don't I?"

"Where does this come from?" I continued to inquire.

"It's just a habit, and I honestly didn't realize it was a thing."

I probed further. "Why do you think it's a habit?"

"He responded, "Because life is hard, and you make things sound so easy, and they're not. Change is painful and not easy."

Immediately, I knew there was something deeper, and my ego was not offended by the fact that James indicated I was the one to make things sound so easy! So, doing what I do, I continue to ask him if we can get to the deeper truth of this statement. Eager to explore the root of this mindset, I led James through a series of mindfulness exercises designed to induce a state of relaxed awareness. As his mind began to quiet and his defenses lowered, we delved into the origins of his belief.

"It's something my dad used to say," James revealed, a note of surprise in his voice as he connected the dots. This seemingly harmless throwaway line had burrowed deep, shaping James's outlook on effort and reward.

Over the following weeks, we worked together to unpack and challenge this inherited belief. James learned to identify and question the automatic responses that had long guided his actions and attitudes through mindfulness and other techniques I taught him.

He learned he was subconsciously adhering to a pattern of struggle, convinced that without pain, work wasn't meaningful. This belief, echoed by a sarcastic mantra "if it were only that easy," masked a deeper conviction that ease was unattainable.

Together, we challenged this notion, and James confronted this inherited belief. He began focusing on embracing ease as not only possible but preferable. This shift in perspective allowed James to redefine his approach to work and life, moving away from a mindset of constant struggle towards one of achievable ease.

He learned that acknowledging effort doesn't necessarily equate to enduring hardship. "I've realized struggle doesn't have to define my experiences. Seeking goals can be harmonious, not just a series of obstacles," James discovered.

This transformation led to a significantly more fulfilling life, proving to James that adopting a mindset of ease can lead to profound personal growth and satisfaction.

Deepening Your Awareness:

Consider moments when nerves led you to say something out of autopilot, later causing self-doubt or self-criticism. Reflect on why your brain reacted that way and what this reveals about your underlying beliefs.

Reflect on habitual responses that may not serve you well, like dismissing suggestions or challenges with phrases like "Yeah, if it were only that easy." Think about the origin of these habits and what they imply about your beliefs regarding effort, change, and success. Of course, if you get stuck, just like my client James, I am here to help guide you through a personalized neuro-performance coaching session if you like. Reach out to hello@heatherjcrider.com to inquire.

Engage in a self-reflective exercise focusing on your automatic responses and beliefs. Ask yourself why you hold certain beliefs and whether they serve your highest good.

Awareness and mindful examination can liberate you from unhelpful patterns, leading to a more fulfilling and authentic life.

Chapter Two

Unshackling Beliefs, Bias, and Behavior

"By three methods we may learn wisdom: first, by reflection, which is noblest; second, by imitation, which is easiest; and third, by experience, which is the most bitter." ~ Confusious

Awareness: The Gateway to Expansion and Healing

Embarking on a journey of self-discovery opens us up to endless possibilities and brings us face-to-face with our past wounds and insecurities. Awareness is that illuminating force that highlights the gaps between our current reality and our aspirations, presenting us with growth opportunities. However, confronting these opportunities often means navigating through a sea of emotions and challenging the limiting beliefs that have held us back.

During a quiet morning meditation, a wave of unease washed over me, a stark reminder of the imposter syndrome that frequently visited me. Imposter syndrome wasn't a new guest; it was a shadow that had loomed over me for years, making me doubt my place in everything I did. It was a constant companion, whispering doubts about my worth and achievements. Instead of being overwhelmed, I decided to recognize this unwelcome visitor for what it was—a deep-seated belief rooted in my subconscious that is part of me but does not define me —which allowed me to acknowledge its presence without letting it derail my day. This moment of awareness, recognizing the depths from which these feelings arose, allowed me to see them for what they were—echoes of old narratives, not dictators of my worth. By letting them be, understanding their roots, and accepting their part in my journey, I found a way to coexist with them, moving forward with a newfound acceptance of myself.

Navigating the Monkey Mind and Embracing Awareness

In our journey of personal growth, it's common to encounter what's often referred to as the "monkey mind" - a term that vividly captures our mind's tendency to jump from thought to thought, especially when trying to get a multitude of tasks and responsibilities. As described earlier, I have had to learn how to co-exist with and manage my monkey mind. This phenomenon is particularly noticeable during high-stress times when our to-do lists and various tasks seem most daunting.

The challenge lies not in the presence of these thoughts but in their potential to distract us from the tools and practices that support our well-being and goals. The more we let these distractions take hold, the more stress and tension build up, leaving us feeling overwhelmed and, metaphorically, with clenched fists.

However, the key to navigating this mental chaos lies in the Reflection ABCs, particularly emphasizing "A" for Awareness. We can examine our attitudes, beliefs, biases, prejudices, values, and habits by fostering awareness. While seemingly daunting, this process is straightforward and can be as simple as questioning why we react in specific ways. Such introspection can lead to profound insights and shifts in perspective.

Psychology, Skepticism, and Societal Negativity

So much of what we have been taught by psychology and society leans heavily towards negativity and doubt, doesn't it?

This idea to spot what is wrong with us is driven by a survival instinct that ironically feeds on self-doubt and thrives on self-criticism. It's like there's a societal script, backed by psychological theories, that's obsessed with labeling every quirk and emotion, casting us into roles of perpetual inadequacy.

In exploring the depths of our societal and psychological conditioning, it's essential to acknowledge the undercurrents of implicit and confirmation biases that silently shape our perceptions and behaviors. Studies illuminate the startling reality of these biases. For instance, research by Amodio et al. (2004) reveals our brains' unconscious associations that link certain groups with fear, showcasing how deeply ingrained and auto-matic these responses can be.

Moreover, as highlighted by Wason & Evans (1975), con-firmation bias demonstrates our tendency to cherry-pick in-formation that aligns with our pre-existing beliefs, further en-trenching us in skewed perceptions. These biases aren't just academic footnotes; they shape our daily lives, steering us to-ward misunderstanding and conflict.

Fast forward to today, and these cognitive quirks are exploit-ed by advertisers, who dazzle us with promises of quick fixes. But skepticism need not mean closing ourselves off. It's about getting smart, asking questions, and not taking things at face value – a balance of doubt and trust that keeps us grounded yet open to new ideas and possibilities.

This tightrope walk between skepticism and open-minded-ness isn't just mental gymnastics; it's crucial in making deci-sions that can seriously impact lives. Going back to our influ-ences, however, because we are more conditioned to focus on what's wrong than what's right, we continue to support the negativity and cognitive biases.

It's wired into us, this knee-jerk reaction to dismiss anything that doesn't fit our worldview, yet there's hope. We have this unique ability to shift our beliefs, to reroute our brain's wiring towards more open-minded shores.

Positive Psychology

Enter Psychologist Dr. Martin Seligman, a beacon of light in the often gloomy realm of psychology. Dr. Seligman is a brilliant psychologist and excellent orator who has extensively challenged this gloomy narrative and miseducation our society has placed around negativity and labeling everything as bad or wrong. He argues for a shift towards 'positive psychology,' a realm where we focus not on our failings but on our potential for happiness, achievement, and genuine connection. Seligman's work shines a light on how our conditioning leans to view ourselves through a lens smeared with negativity, and he offers a different path—one that's about recognizing our strengths, our capacity for growth, and the undeniable power of positive emotion.

Seligman surmised that the original measure of life satisfaction boiled down to the five pillars of well-being - positive emotion, engagement, meaning, positive relationships, and accomplishment. Or the PERMA model.

It's time to question this old script, to wonder why we've been so quick to accept a narrative that dims our light rather than fuels our fire. Why have we allowed these negative beliefs to dictate our self-image and possibilities? Recognizing and challenging these ingrained perceptions is the first step toward rewriting our stories, not with the ink of past traumas and societal judgments, but with the vibrant colors of our own choosing.

Evolution Through Awareness

Understanding our own evolution deeply intertwines with becoming aware of our thoughts and beliefs. Through my journey and in guiding hundreds of clients, I've seen firsthand how recognizing the roots of our beliefs is pivotal. For example, noticing that my hesitation in meetings stemmed not from shyness but from a belief that my ideas weren't valuable was a breakthrough. Acknowledging such patterns is the first step towards change. It's not merely about identifying these patterns but understanding their origins and consciously choosing to evolve past them. This evolution isn't just about overcoming past labels or diagnoses; it's about harnessing awareness to transform our internal narratives and achieve our true goals and desires. Such awareness allows us to shift from being stuck in a cycle of negative emotion to embracing a path of success, happiness, and well-being, proving that the key to significant impact lies in knowing and addressing the why behind our behaviors.

Internal Beliefs Affecting Interactions

Think about this another way. Every day, our inner beliefs subtly guide our actions, from how we talk to a partner to negotiating with our boss. These beliefs often act like a background script, influencing us without conscious input. They're like glasses through which we view the world, coloring our perceptions and interactions based on past programming and experiences. This lens can open us up to growth or cage us in cycles of doubt and limitation.

For example, say I need to approach an employee about paying more attention to detail when she is writing a report. I might assume she will feel offended; therefore, I approach her in a certain way, affecting my communication. Or say you want to ask your boss for a raise and assume you are not worthy because of a preconscious belief about money. Therefore, you approach with a particular assumption, or you don't ask at all.

Or consider this: If I ask my son to help me pick up the kitchen, I might ask in a frustrated tone because I already believe he will whine and respond with resistance. From experience, he usually whines and resists, so I'm most likely correct in my assessment. How I approach him is already determined by my beliefs about my feelings and how he will respond. Instead of simply asking without a feeling attached to it, I am approaching him already with a specific emotion.

Whatever the situation, the lens through which you see will affect how you feel and approach others.

Another example: Recently, I had a conversation with a dear friend, Sarah. Her oldest child was going through some challenges adjusting to a new world, admitting and living as a gay woman. When Sarah explained to some of her other friends and social circle about what her daughter was experiencing, the friends immediately defaulted to judgment, prejudice, and rejection. "How could they treat Sarah this way for something her daughter was experiencing, especially something personal and also somewhat traumatic in parts of society?" Sarah and her daughter are the most unique, kind, loving, and mindful people. For their social circle to treat them unkindly was a pure insult. Everyone is entitled to an opinion. But what lens and filter are people running their opinions through? Have they asked themselves what their beliefs are and why?

These situations can be controversial in some ways because they can be deeply personal. Many people default to unkind thoughts or negative behavior towards people who present themselves differently. But why? What is really behind the prejudice and negativity?

I recall a situation with a client, Kenny, several years ago. I met Kenny through another colleague, and he was a very well-respected businessman in the community. I knew I could help him, and he needed a lot of guidance with his business. I sat with him in several meetings, and he never looked me in the eye. He was curt and almost rude when I called him on the phone. Once, he called another colleague and claimed I sat at his kitchen table and demanded a cup of coffee. I never asked for one nor had a cup of coffee in his kitchen. But I kept moving forward, interacting with him, believing I could help him. However, there came a point in this process when I realized his beliefs were too entrenched for me to overcome. He was an older white male, and I was a younger female. He didn't look me in the eye because he held a prejudice that women were not capable of, nor should be, in the workplace. Observing a few interactions with his wife and daughter clarified this. He showed me no respect and did not believe I could achieve what he wanted, even though he kept taking my meetings because he had hope in what he wanted to accomplish, and I was the only one presenting the solution correctly.

This prejudice was not unfamiliar to me, especially when I was younger. There is a bias that women are not as bright and men should do business with men and that women are not as capable as men. I faced a choice once I realized that this client was firmly set in his prejudice. I could attempt to change his mind or let him go as a client. I believed I could help him and was proposing precisely what he needed. He agreed with what I was proposing, but his disbelief in me as a female was too strong for him to accept my help.

Therefore, I asked a male colleague, Mike, to partner with me when deciding how to move forward. I knew my solution was correct, and Mike could reassure Kenny. Guess what, it worked. Kenny moved forward, not with me, but with Mike. Kenny didn't know that I was instructing Mike the entire time on the goals and actions to take. I eventually let Mike handle Kenny exclusively to avoid any potential conflict. Looking back at this situation, if I were to encounter it today, I would not have accepted Kenny as a client or gone through the effort to involve Mike. My belief in myself and how I could serve was solid and even more solid now. I've learned that sometimes you must realize some people will not change their beliefs. However, given the opportunity, I might opt out for my own sanity next time!

In the workplace and when dealing with others in teams, it is crucial to understand how people show up with their beliefs. It aids in navigating and attempting to collaborate with them.

Understanding and acknowledging everyone's biases and prejudices is crucial for effective communication and teamwork. Recognizing that our interactions begin with our perspectives—shaped by biases, beliefs, and prejudices—enables us to approach others more thoughtfully. This self-awareness allows for more successful collaborations by considering not only what we believe but also how we convey these beliefs. Emphasizing the importance of reflecting on our biases can lead to more constructive outcomes in every situation, enhancing our ability to work together towards common goals.

At the end of the day, we choose our beliefs. Understanding that our initial default reactions usually come from the lens we currently run our experiences through and then react to is power.

Because our default is our lens, we must challenge ourselves. We get challenged often by others, but how often do you stop and thoroughly reflect on your beliefs, patterns, habits, lens through which you see, and where they come from? To honestly examine their origin and why you believe what you do. Not just to gain a neurological understanding but to seek to understand where, in your lifetime, these beliefs formed.

As implied earlier, the brain undergoes the most development from ages two to eight. We are sponges at these ages. How many times have you said or heard how babies are "just sponges soaking up everything they come in contact with?"

Everything we see and everything we observe becomes part of our belief system and our value system and forms who we are.

We observe behaviors and habits from others, then repeat them, and they become patterns. Sometimes, we encounter a setback that causes us to look at our beliefs, but then we get into a blame-shame-guilt cycle. And that's just a useless cycle. We take it personally because our decisions always lead us to where we are.

But I don't want to!

I have a very opinionated friend. Of course, we are all opinionated in our ways, but she knows she is opinionated and doesn't want to change. No matter the situation or conversation, she believes her way and viewpoints are correct. No matter what.

And she will tell you as much, too. If I offer her another perspective and way of viewing a situation, she will quickly reply with a firm response that reminds me that she is just stuck in her beliefs, and that is that!

Her belief is her belief because she has decided that she doesn't want to change. She doesn't want her brain to recreate how she sees and views life. It's not her fault, though. It's her brain's fault. The brain doesn't like to change. The brain likes routine and for patterns to remain the same. Remaining in the same patterns keeps the brain nice and happy and comfortable to stay in primary survival mode.

We all have unconscious bias that shows up when we interact with others. Our brain needs to process information quickly; this is the survival-driven mechanism, specifically the emotional regulation network, part of the limbic system.

Part of our automatic reaction response. The brain learns how to shortcut thinking and decision-making based on past experiences, forming a bias. Of course, not all biases are wrong. However, these past experiences or memories often create an unconscious thought pattern that affects a decision or interaction.

Do you have a brain? If so, you have biases and patterns for prejudice and patterns of belief.

We must learn how to slow down and create a different kind of thought filter to connect our intuitive and cognitive thinking to ensure we make decisions with as little bias and through the most present awareness.

Neuroscience-Backed Strategies

The common misconception about our brains is that we lose brain cells as we age, making us less capable of change. Neuroscience reveals that our brains are not fixed but are capable of remarkable change, a concept known as Neuroplasticity. This understanding opens up robust pathways for overcoming limiting beliefs and biases. Dr. Shad Helmstetter, author of Neuroplasticity, offers teachings on Neuroplasticity and highlights how practices like self-compassion and positive affirmations can activate parts of the brain involved in learning and memory, fostering the rewiring of neural pathways to support more empowering beliefs.

Visualization also plays a crucial role in this transformation. Engaging in guided visualization in a state of relaxed, mindful awareness can enhance Neuroplasticity, strengthening the connection between positive emotions and our aspirations. This process allows us to "see" and "feel" our desired outcomes, embedding these optimistic scenarios deep within our neural networks.

Gratitude is another potent tool in reshaping our brains. Regular gratitude meditation shifts our focus towards positivity, gradually weakening the grip of limiting beliefs. By consistently practicing gratitude, we train our brain to recognize and appreciate the positive aspects of our lives, fostering a mindset that supports growth, well-being, and achieving our goals. My article in Brainz magazine, Titled "The Neurological Magic of Gratitude: Transforming Brain Bonds and Business",[1] discusses how the neuroscience of gratitude is instrumental in improving mental and physical health, fostering effective workplace communication, and enhancing productivity.

Incorporating neuroscience-backed strategies into our daily routines can lead to profound changes in how we think, feel, and interact with the world, demonstrating the incredible adaptability and resilience of the human brain.

The Journey of Self-Discovery and Neural Rewiring

This approach to personal growth is not just about managing stress or overcoming distractions; it's a profound journey of self-discovery and neural rewiring. By consistently engaging in practices that promote awareness, establishing non-negotiables, and utilizing intention questions, we're not only combating the immediate challenges posed by our monkey mind but also fundamentally transforming how we perceive and interact with the world around us.

The ultimate goal is to create a reality that resonates with our deepest values and desires, leveraging the incredible power of our brain to shape our experiences and outcomes. Through mindful awareness and intentional action, we can navigate life's complexities with grace, building a foundation of resilience and positivity that supports our journey toward fulfillment and well-being.

---

1. https://www.brainzmagazine.com/post/the-neurological-magic-of-g ratitude-transforming-brain-bonds-and-business

Chapter Summary:

Awareness as a Foundation: By highlighting the importance of self-awareness in identifying and understanding our deep-seated beliefs and biases, we often find the root causes of our limitations and struggles.

Challenging Negative Conditioning: This demonstrates how society and psychology have historically focused on the negative, encouraging us to examine and challenge these ingrained perceptions to foster personal growth.

Positive Psychology's Role: Dr. Martin Seligman's positive psychology concept emphasizes focusing on strengths, growth, and the positive aspects of life as a counterbalance to traditional negative bias.

Impact of Internal Beliefs on Interactions: Our internal beliefs and biases shape our interactions with others, often subconsciously, and stresses the need for mindfulness in our communications and relationships.

Neuroscience and Change: Neuroscience-backed strategies, such as Neuroplasticity, visualization, and gratitude, demonstrate our brain's capacity for change and the power of positive thinking and beliefs.

Unshackling Beliefs, Bias, and Behavior is a comprehensive guide to understanding and transforming our beliefs and biases. It blends personal insight with psychological and neurological research to encourage you to reflect on your internal narratives, challenge negative conditioning, and adopt strategies for positive change.

Through awareness, positive psychology, and neuroscience, we are shown a path toward more fulfilling interactions and a more empowered approach to life.

Go Reflect Yourself Reflection Exercise: Awareness of Habits

Change your glasses and wear a few different pairs.

Recall a situation where you and another individual were misaligned. Misalignment is how I describe when two people are not in agreement or on the same page.

Write down some of the details of this situation.

Think about how you approached the situation.

Think about how you viewed how they approached the situation.

Now ask yourself:

- What kind of belief, bias, story, filter, or lens have you looked through in this situation that could have caused part of this misalignment?

- Did you have a situation in the past with someone who looked like this individual that caused you to immediately think something about them was untrue?

- Did you immediately assume something untrue due to a belief about yourself?

- Did you have an old partner who used to say something similar that just ticked you off, and you immediately decided with this situation to relate the two people together? Maybe you were so determined to achieve something that your bias was to be closed-minded to the other person.

- Stop and reflect on this situation and if any stories, old biases, or beliefs could have affected your baseline filter with this scenario.

- Now ask yourself: If you were the other person, what could have been going on in their life or during this situation that could have caused them to think or feel a certain way? What potential filter could they have been looking through during this misalignment?

Many circumstances cause misalignment.
- If you were to approach this situation again knowing what you now know, how could you approach it differently?

Take a moment to consider your daily habits, starting with something as routine as your morning rituals.

Reflect on these questions:
- What habits have shaped your life?

- Who has influenced these habits, and do they reflect who you want to be?

BONUS REFLECTION:

Dive Deeper with Your Money Story:

Consider your attitudes toward money, shaped by early experiences.

Think back to your childhood:

- What beliefs about money were expressed by those around you?

- How have these beliefs affected your view of success, wealth, and financial management?

Challenge Your Beliefs:

Our beliefs, often formed early in life, can significantly influence our present decisions and interactions. It's crucial to question these ingrained perceptions:

- What common phrases or beliefs about money have influenced you?

- Are these beliefs serving your current goals and well-being?

Understanding Bias and Prejudice:

Recognize that external influences shape our internal beliefs. Reflecting on our biases allows us to move forward with greater awareness.

- What bias do you feel you have? Why?

- How can you approach life differently knowing these biases exist?

Final Reflection:

This exercise encourages you to "change your glasses" and view situations through various lenses, fostering empathy and understanding in your interactions.

- Reflect on how a shift in perspective could transform misalignments into opportunities for growth and connection.

- What additional insights and takeaways did you gain from this chapter?

Chapter Three

The Path to Deservability

"There is no passion to be found in settling for a life that is less than the one you are capable of living."
~Nelson Mandela

For years, a particular house seemed to whisper my name each time I passed by. Nestled against an open field, with a backdrop of a tree-lined creek, something about it captivated me. Often, as I walked by, I wondered about its interior, which, from the outside, seemed to blend with the neighborhood yet stood out to me. One day, the universe conspired to unlock its doors for me as I heard a rumor that it was going up for sale. Immediately, I contacted the owner, whom I knew, and she eagerly invited me over. Stepping inside as I crossed the threshold, I felt a rush of excitement similar to that feeling that came from finally seeing that long-awaited movie in the theater. Yet, a shadow crept over me as we walked through the house together, and she narrated the love and laughter that filled those spaces.

The house was everything I had dreamed of - grand yet inviting, a perfect canvas for my family's memories. But a voice inside me whispered, "You don't belong here." Despite being financially viable and timely, my internal beliefs overshadowed my logic and desire, which were silenced by a deep-seated belief that I hadn't earned the right to this happiness, this piece of the world.

In the end, I chose another house. Comfortable, yet not the one that had captured my heart. I told myself the screened porch tipped the scales - a feature my dream house lacked. But the truth was, the porch was just a metaphor for my own feelings of inadequacy. Deep down, I felt unworthy of the house that had spoken to me, inferior, as if its walls were too grand for someone like me. I remember saying to myself, "You're not ready." That experience remains a poignant reminder of the battles we fight within ourselves, the stories we tell ourselves about what we deserve and why. It's a chapter in my own story that I revisit often, wondering how different the narrative might have been if I had believed I was enough for that house, for that dream.

This feeling of 'deserving' is not unfamiliar to me. It has been a recurring theme in my life, manifesting in various scenarios. As a young adult, I desired a $200 watch but felt I needed to achieve a particular milestone before deserving it. This self-imposed barrier prevented me from purchasing the watch, despite affording more expensive items, because I had tied its acquisition to a sense of deservability that I continuously moved. This pattern extended to vacations, meals, events, and relationships, constantly feeling undeserving. What lies behind this feeling? A lack of self-belief, self-worth, feelings of inadequacy, or comparison?

Numerous factors contribute to our perceptions of what we deserve and don't deserve. On the journey toward self-empowerment and realizing our deepest desires, the major obstacle often lies within our perceptions of what we believe we deserve.

Imagine navigating a forest shrouded in the fog of doubts and fears, where each step is uncertain due to our ingrained beliefs about worthiness. In the quiet of these woods, we learn that achieving our goals is not just about wanting; it's about believing—not only in the possibility but also in our deservingness of that possibility.

"Believe you deserve it, and the universe will serve it."

Because most of our programming comes from past experiences, you may not even know the underlying belief when you feel you do or do not deserve something.

Imagine standing at the edge of a new venture, heart pounding with anticipation and a whisper of doubt clouding your thoughts. I was on the brink of a decision that could redefine my career. The leap from comfortable predictability to the unknown was daunting, not because I doubted my abilities but because I questioned my deservability of success.

There are differences between your belief in your ability to do something, or your ability to belong somewhere, and your belief in your feeling of deserving of someone or something. Just as in my story above about the house I turned down, I believed I could live there, and I believed I could afford it; however, I did not believe I belonged.

While talking with a colleague I met a few years ago, we discussed feeling deserving. We had a long plane ride to get to the training we attended, and he said he did not go to the airport Delta lounge because he felt he did not belong there. I had not thought about it before and asked him what he meant. He said, "I don't know, I'm not super successful, nor super rich, so I just didn't feel like I belonged."

Why does being rich or having a certain level of success determine whether you belong to an airport lounge? As discussed in the prior chapter, because of our own brains, society's labels, bias, or prejudice might lead us to feel and believe in such. I remember feeling the same way the first time I visited an airport. I had lounge access for years before realizing I could take advantage of it and enjoy some of its pleasures and comforts. But I had a subconscious mindset that I didn't deserve such luxuries.

Understanding deservability extends beyond simply accepting that we deserve the best in life; it involves a profound recognition of our intrinsic value and capabilities. Neuroscience reveals that our brain's wiring significantly shapes our self-perception and influences our decisions and behaviors. Fortunately, this wiring is not immutable but flexible through neuroplasticity, indicating that we can adjust our self-view toward a more positive outlook through intentional effort.

At the core of deservability is the idea that our worth does not depend on external achievements or validation but is a fundamental part of who we are. Acknowledging this is vital as it impacts all areas of our lives, from our ambitions to our relationships. By fully understanding and embracing our inherent worth, we unlock a more genuine and empowered version of ourselves.

Imposter Syndrome

Imagine standing on a stage, spotlight glaring down, with an audience of peers and mentors waiting to hear your insights. Yet, as you look out, chilling thoughts of doubt creep in: "Do I truly belong here?" "I'm not accomplished enough," "I don't deserve to be here," "What if they think I'm a fraud?" This is the essence of imposter syndrome. It's like wearing a mask, fearing the moment it might slip and reveal you as an impostor or some other version you are desperately attempting to conceal. Despite milestones, achievements, and many happy clients, there is a persistent belief that your success is unmerited, un-earned, or unwarranted as if a product of something else rather than skill.

Conversations feel like tightrope walks, where any moment could expose a perceived lack of knowledge or ability. This shadow of doubt, even during success, can make you feel per-petually out of place, burdened by the weight of perceived inadequacy.

Imposter syndrome, the belief that you're not as competent as others perceive you to be, can be a significant barrier to feeling deserving.

I encounter imposter syndrome on a daily basis but usually don't realize it at first. Talking with my stylist this week, I was talking about this book, and the first thing I said was that I hope what I am writing is valuable, but I'm not so sure. She picked up on the nuances of what I was saying and immedi-ately started sharing stories of her own where her gut reaction was to have self-doubt. I then realized my own belief in how

I communicated the very book I am writing about belief. Oh, the irony of life! This is human and natural, too. It's not that we won't have these feelings; it's about catching them and what to do with them when we realize we are experiencing them.

A few simple ways to help understand that imposter syndrome is a common experience is first to understand that it is not a personal failure.

Strategies to explore, which we will discuss in more detail in a later chapter, include talking about your feelings with trusted peers, practicing self-compassion, and setting realistic expectations for yourself.

Ultimately, however, the goal is to create a deeper sense of worthiness by removing some of the effects imposter syndrome has on your actions.

The more worth you feel about yourself, the more free you are to pursue and attempt to accomplish your goals.

In essence, Your net worth = self-worth.

Cultivating a Mindset of Worthiness

Neuroscience provides evidence that our thought patterns, influenced by our perception of worth, can be rewired through practices like mindfulness, positive affirmations, and cognitive behavioral strategies. This process of reprogramming our thoughts to foster a positive self-view is similar to training a muscle; it requires consistency and dedication. By engaging in these practices, we not only enhance our sense of deservability but also our overall mental and emotional well-being.

In essence, understanding deservability is about recognizing and nurturing the value within ourselves. It's about changing the narrative from one of self-doubt and limitation to one of empowerment and possibility. Through this understanding, we pave the way for a life that reflects our true worth and capabilities, emboldened by the knowledge that we deserve every good thing that comes our way.

Deservability Quotient

Walking down the path to understanding deservability starts with a foundation of self-acceptance, recognizing our worth, and celebrating our achievements. Yet, the journey is often colored by the subjective lenses of 'deservedness,' a spectrum ranging from healthy to unhealthy perceptions.

The "Deservability Quotient" is a concept I've devised to gauge how deeply we believe in our worth and our entitlement to success. This quotient, blending self-perception with the hurdles and uncertainties life throws at us, serves as a personal barometer to assess our feelings of deservability amidst an immediate situation or challenge we may be facing. It's not just a measure but a reality check, inviting us to reflect on where we stand and where we aim to be.

Elevating this quotient is a dynamic process, requiring you to engage in deep self-reflection, celebrate your victories—big and small—and confront the shadows of doubt, such as imposter syndrome. This isn't merely an exercise in self-improvement; it's a transformative process that reinforces your belief in your inherent values and capabilities. This process enhances your conviction in deserving the best in life, mirroring the concept that nurturing your self-worth directly influences your capacity to recognize, attain, and retain success.

During a recent reflection, I thought, "I don't deserve a break because I took time off recently." This is an unhealthy view because when I'm tired, I deserve a break, and sometimes, my own internal belief that I must work 24 hours a day overrides my reality of self-care. I love to work, but sometimes, I am hard on myself when not working. My Deservability Quotient here was low, indicative of a harsh self-assessment.

Conversely, when I explained to my son that he didn't deserve video game time due to unfinished homework, it demonstrated a healthier perspective of deservability that underscores responsibility and agreements. Despite not receiving what he desired, this approach wasn't about diminishing his worth but reinforcing the importance of responsibility. Although I caught myself and removed the word 'deserve.' I rephrased it and said, you don't get any video time simply because you didn't do your homework.

However, to keep his perspective realistic and strengthen his worth, I also surprise my son with gifts and treats from time to time, like eating out or his favorite donuts, to reinforce that not every reward must be earned through specific achievement. I want him to know that he can have treats, surprises, or rewards because he's my son, and I love him. This practice reinforces the belief that he deserves simply for being himself, a fantastic human, and highlights a healthy view of deservability that separates intrinsic worth from accomplishments.

Sometimes, I believe we get too involved in wanting gold stars to prove our value or worth when our actual worth lies in simply being an incredible human. Too much is attached to needing to prove accomplishment in order to deserve and be rewarded with treats or experiences. I am all for attaching a treat or experience as a reward for an accomplishment. Still, there needs to be a healthy boundary between how we view ourselves as deserving versus a simple reward for an accomplishment.

This nuanced understanding of deservability, distinguishing between healthy and unhealthy perceptions, is crucial for fostering self-worth and navigating the complexity and dynamics of situations.

To further illustrate.

A client, Taryn, approached me a few years ago to work through her business goals, her current reality, and her desired future reality. We looked at the things that are currently in her way and identified a key obstacle: her belief that worthiness was tied to constant work, a mindset inherited from her business-owning parents who equated struggle with effort.

Her parents owned businesses and were always working and saying things such as, "You always struggle as a business owner" or "If you're not struggling, you're not trying hard enough."

Despite recognizing this detrimental belief, Taryn grappled with allowing herself to relax and find peace outside of work, leading to a low Deservability Quotient. Her deep-seated beliefs manifested as stress and struggle in her business, hindering her ability to achieve her goals.

This persistent belief led to an array of self-imposed problems, manifesting stress and a sense of constant battle rooted in the conviction that she must endure hardship to deserve success. Taryn's situation was a textbook example of how ingrained beliefs and subconscious patterns deeply influence our sense of deservability.

She knew that her parent's influence existed and that she did not want to carry this same amount of negativity.

Taryn's situation involved many factors of belief, and her subconscious patterns ran deep, not unlike most of us. Because her overall deservability remained relatively low, maybe a constant 50, she had difficulty achieving the goals, freedom, and peace she desired.

Taryn began to shift her outlook upon understanding her Deservability Quotient. She created a new filter for herself, adopting the new belief that her baseline starts with the viewpoint that she is a deserving person. In turn, she slowly shifted her perspective—that she deserves peace, love, freedom, joy, and success without relentless' work.' She learned to challenge her thoughts and feelings about what she deserves, gradually improving her self-worth and overall deservability.

Because her habits and patterns run deep, her deservability quotient is her Northstar to help her when challenged. As her quotient goes down, she reminds herself to test her thoughts and underlying feelings about how she views what she deserves by her quotient. This will remind her and keep her moving into a more optimistic viewpoint, consistently increasing how she values her self-worth.

Look at everything you do that supports and enhances or increases your deservability quotient.

When your deservability quotient comes from a position of self-loathing and self-deprecation, you are fueling the inner imposter. When you increase your deservability quotient and strengthen your position to one of self-value, self-worth, and self-compassion, you can start to change your default state to a more positive one with peace and harmony.

As we nurture our self-worth, our conviction in our deservability strengthens, directly impacting our ability to recognize, achieve, and sustain success. This process doesn't just change how we see ourselves; it changes how we interact with the world around us, empowering us to claim the life we seek and truly deserve.

Recognizing your inherent worth sets the stage for the Deservability Quotient, yet knowing is only the first step. You must transform this knowledge into belief through action to truly elevate this quotient. Here, affirmations come into play, serving not just as reminders but as tools to reshape our self-perception and reinforce our belief in our deservability of success and happiness. I know, I know, affirmations seem cheesy, right?! Trust me, the brain needs positive reinforcement.

According to neuroscience, when you employ affirmations, they can trigger positive feelings and reinforce your desired identity. Brain scans show that when people practice affirmations, there is increased activity in the area of the brain that is involved in the positive self-evaluation and reward centers (ventromedial prefrontal cortex).[1] The concept of neuroplasticity, which we mentioned earlier and will further discuss in Chapter 4, also suggests that affirmations might positively strengthen neural connections toward positive goals and weaken associated negativity.

Deservability Declarations:

Putting into action:

After identifying areas where our Deservability Quotient may falter—like my moment of self-doubt about deserving a break—we can employ specific affirmations tailored to counteract these doubts. This method extends the foundational understanding of our worth into a practical, daily practice that actively boosts our Deservability Quotient.

A Powerful tool to use is Deservability Declarations. These are not mere affirmations but profound commitments to oneself, articulating a deep-seated belief in one's worthiness of love, success, happiness, and abundance. Through these declarations, you engage in an intimate dialogue with your subconscious, reprogramming the narratives that have held you back.

Imagine a story where the protagonist, faced with a reflection of their doubts, chooses instead to affirm their worthiness. Each declaration becomes a step forward on their path, illuminating the forest with the light of self-belief. This is the essence of the journey toward deservability—it's about shifting the narrative from one of limitation to one of limitless potential and possibility, everything we have discussed to this point.

When you are emphatic about your worth, you are powerful in how you declare your worth. You are reinforcing to your subconscious that this is serious, and you are ready to feel worthy.

The Quotient:

I created an entire deservability declaration quotient in one of my programs. If you would like a copy, simply email me at hello@heatherjcrider.com and write in the subject deservability, and I'll be happy to send you a copy.

You can create your own version as well. Here is essentially how the deservability quotient declarations work:

A deservability declaration is a powerful statement that declares your commitment to embracing worthiness and deservingness of all aspects of a fulfilling life. It involves a conscious decision to release inherited or self-imposed limitations and an affirmation of your right to love success, health, and abundance. This declaration is not just an affirmation but a commitment to yourself to take actionable steps toward realizing your desired reality. It signifies a pivotal moment of acknowledgment that you are worthy of your dreams and aspirations, not because of any external validation or achievement but simply because of your inherent value as a being. It's a transformative tool designed to align your self-perception with your highest potential, enabling you to manifest your goals and desires effectively.

To establish new patterns to focus your thoughts and attention on creating your new reality. Reframe your negative and old thinking into new, empowering thoughts that serve your desired future reality.

It's time to declare you as deserving.

Create Your Own Statements Below (see example).

Once you have completed yours...get yourself in a relaxed, mindful awareness state and read this declaration out loud while looking at yourself in a mirror! Declare it.

Own it. Become It...Because You Deserve It!

For example:
- I release and let go of the limitations of my parents and those who have influenced me.

- I love them and allow myself to go beyond them.

- I am not their negative opinions nor their limiting beliefs.

- I am not bound by any of the fears or prejudices of my current society.

- I no longer identify with limitations of any kind.

- In my mind, I have total freedom.

- I now move into a new space of consciousness where I am willing to see myself differently.

- I am worthy. I am deserving.

- I deserve to receive ALL my good.

- I am eager to empower myself to create new thoughts about my life.

- My new thinking becomes my new experience.

- I now know and affirm the universe conspires in my favor, and as such, I now prosper in a number of ways.

- The totality of prosperity lies before me.

- I deserve life. I deserve an abundant and good life. I deserve my desired reality.

- I deserve love and an abundance of love. I deserve good health and well-being.

- I deserve to live comfortably with abundance and prosperity.

Deservability for teams and organizations:

Imagine bringing the concept of deservability into the heart of your business and team. Picture each member of your team, each with their unique sense of value and trust within the group. Now, think about the magic of amplifying their Deservability Quotient. It's like igniting a spark within them, boosting their confidence and trust in the collective vision.

They become more engaged and eager to collaborate and share innovative ideas. It's about acknowledging everyone's worth and making them feel seen and valued. When we adopt and share these values, we work and thrive together. By fostering an environment where everyone feels their deservability is recognized, you can create a culture of openness, trust, and empowerment. This isn't just about enhancing productivity; it's about transforming our workplace into a vibrant, creative hub where everyone feels like they truly belong and can contribute their best.

Chapter Summary:

Remember that the path to deservability is ongoing. Each step forward, each moment of recognition, adds to the foundation of your self-belief in exploring its critical role in self-empowerment and the achievement of our deepest desires.

We've uncovered that deservability extends beyond simply believing in being worthy of the best life offers. It requires a profound acknowledgment of our inherent worth and a commitment to overcoming the barriers that shadow our belief in ourselves, such as imposter syndrome.

It's essential to recognize that the path to fully realizing our deservability is not a destination but a continuous process of growth and self-reflection. Each step taken towards recognizing our worth, each moment of overcoming doubt, and every practice of mindfulness and positive affirmation adds layers to our foundation of self-belief. This journey is about transforming our narrative from one constrained by self-doubt and perceived limitations to one that celebrates our limitless potential and inherent worthiness.

Embrace your journey towards deservability with the understanding that you are not alone in this quest. The realization that we deserve every good thing that comes our way is a powerful acknowledgment of our humanity and a testament to our resilience. Let this chapter be a stepping stone towards a life where your dreams are not just possibilities but inevitable outcomes of your belief in your deservedness. Embrace your worthiness with open arms, and let it guide you toward your dreams.

Go Reflect Yourself Reflection Exercise: Deservability Reflection

Pause and reflect on your journey. Consider your achievements, the challenges you've overcome, and the growth you've experienced.

- What are three moments in your life where you felt proud of yourself?

- How do these moments reflect your inherent worthiness?

- In what ways can you remind yourself of your deservability daily?

- Create your own deservability statements and/or email hello@heatherjcrider.com for a worksheet to help you create one.

- What do you think your current deservability quotient is?

- What is contributing to this number?

- What quotient do you want?

- How can you achieve this number?

- What additional reflections or insights have you gained?

Chapter Four

Overcoming Obstacles and Achieving Goals

"Obstacles are those frightful things you see when you take your eyes off your goal." ~Henry Ford

"Aren't you tired of being so strong all the time?" A friend recently asked me after I told him about a colossal scam I fell for recently.

One morning, I had not yet had my morning supplements nor meditated and was still sleepy. This is my way of saying my brain was not fully awake, and I was distracted. When I received a call from a loved one, he said frantically, "Some cryptocurrency fraud has hacked my Etsy account, and I am on the other line with the fraud department, and they're going to help me get my money back; can I patch you in and have you help too?"

Of course, immediately, I said yes, without batting an eye. Because that's what you do when someone you love says I need your help. The scammers were clearly seasoned and trained, and they hooked me perfectly. Before I knew it, we were transferring money back and forth and totally convinced the money would be replaced. I felt like I was drinking through a fire hose, and then, at some point, I realized, what a minute, this is not legitimate. Unfortunately, I realized this too late and roped my Uncle into this scam. He was suspicious but went along with it for a minute because I, too, called him frantic, asking for his help. Wow, what a scheme. They had their system down pat. They knew precisely what button to push, what to say, how to ask for money, and they kept reminding me why we were doing this because someone I love was in trouble and needed my help. I was confused, and because I was disoriented, I fell for it, hook-line-and-sinker.

All week, I kept thinking, I should have done this, or I should have done that. I should have realized the moment they said this, or they said that I should have known and should have slammed the phone down. I've beat myself up at times over this. All in all, we lost about $14,000 and had no chance of recovering this money. Compared to a lot of other horror stories, we are perhaps lucky, but the truth is, this situation sucks. It was embarrassing, and I felt stupid. I especially felt stupid because I study the brain, and I know how the brain responds in these situations. My brain reacted exactly the way the scammers hoped it would. I was confused, tired, and distracted, and because of the key phrase, 'my loved one needs your help,' my emotions took over. You will hear a lot of common points and phrases repeated throughout this book because understanding how the brain gets hijacked will help you when your brain gets hijacked!

Inside the limbic system of the brain, in the middle part of the brain located essentially above your ears in the temporal lobe, lies the amygdala, which is essentially the brain's emotional regulation center. This is the area of the brain where emotions flow through to see if something is a threat. It's the flight or fight response center. The sole function here is survival. It seeks pleasure and avoids pain. The flip side of this beautiful survival mechanism is that when the brain gets hijacked, you can become disoriented because of a lag in thinking. This means that when you get hijacked, the front part of your brain, the central executive network, or the prefrontal cortex gets put in a time-out! Think about this part of your brain in your forehead as the brain's CEO or logical decision-maker. When it's in time out, and the emotions are heightened, you're essentially in autopilot mode, as addressed in Chapter 1. Therefore, you are more susceptible to following directions someone else gives you because, at this moment, your logical thinking is essentially and momentarily stunted.

In my case, I was disoriented and I was confused; I wanted to help, and my emotions were already heightened (which is common in our high-stress world), and I was very distracted. Therefore, I fell for the scam, and my brain's decision-making system couldn't escape its temporary 'time out' state.

Now, knowing how this happens and why it happens doesn't help when you are in the middle of such high stress or high trauma. And it doesn't make the situation suck any less! For me, since I do KNOW this is how the brain functions, I felt even more dumb.

Unexpected Obstacles

What happens when struck with serious obstacles or major conflicts?

As a new mother, I was interrupted by a tragic phone call on my first Mother's Day. My sister, who is my only sibling, had been rushed to the hospital. She had been beaten so badly by her husband that she was put on life support and placed into a medically induced coma. Imagine the intensity of this shock and the array of emotions I faced. As a new mother trying to balance my baby, my business, and myself, I now needed to refocus my energy on my sister. When I got to the hospital to see her, I was devastated. It was as if I had just walked into a movie set and was now one of the main characters trying to navigate this tragedy. To make it worse, because of the serious-ness of her situation, she was placed in a protective lockdown at the hospital, and I became the only designated person who was able to visit her, communicate with the hospital, and make decisions on her behalf. Since I was just a new mother, I was way over my head already; now, having the responsibility of my sister's life was almost too much for me to bear.

Every day for six weeks, I would take my baby to the hospital, where my aunt and Uncle would meet me and take her in her carriage for walks around the hospital campus. My Uncle George would sing to her "You are my sunshine"...and they would have the best time while I was in aguish visiting my sister. Then, the moment I reconnected with my daughter, aunt, and Uncle, I put back on my brave face and got back to work and down to business. I kept saying, "I have to keep it together. I cannot lose it. My daughter needs me, my clients need me, and I just have to keep moving forward."

I'm sure I didn't navigate as gracefully as I remember. No, in fact, I know I didn't at all. I was an emotional mess. I canceled client meetings, yelled at my other family members who were around me, and just did what I could to get by. Not knowing if my sister was going to live or die was a near-impossible emotional time for me.

She did survive this incident. But not without deep emotional scars for her, her children, and me.

This is what everyday life is about. An obstacle that you don't expect to exist appears out of nowhere. One day, you are happily gliding through the streams on the river of life, and the next day, a giant boulder comes out of nowhere, and you slam right into it.

Sometimes, these challenges come at you as giant boulders; sometimes, they are small pebbles. Whatever obstacle or interference you encounter can significantly affect you and your life. Muhammad Ali is quoted as saying, "It isn't the mountains ahead to climb that wear you out; it's the pebble in your shoe."

It took me years to understand how to navigate such challenges. Looking back on my life, I have had more obstacles, tragedies, challenges, and stumbling blocks than most people would ever guess. I've joked for years that if I wrote a book about my family and the real events that have happened, people would not believe any of it and call me a fraud, assuming I stole a soap opera script! Maybe someday I will write that book, but maybe not too. All joking aside, life happens. Obstacles occur. Tragedy happens. And fun and exciting things happen, too.

Just as your brain can get hijacked because of tragic and stressful situations, your brain can get equally hijacked due to fun and exciting moments. A new love. A new house. An upcoming trip. Your brain can get hijacked by emotional times and situations for many reasons. Take my daughter as an example. She is 19 years old and has fallen 'in love' several times during her teenage years. I've caught myself asking her why she's made some of the decisions she has, then realizing the moment I ask this question, I answer myself, "Oh yes, it's her brain hijack, and she cannot help herself." At this young age, her brain is still forming, and the intensity of emotions is challenging to manage, especially when dealing with first-time emotional experiences such as teenage boyfriends.

Brain Hijack

Neuroscience Digression

To understand what I mean by all of this, let me quickly digress and expand further about the neuroscience behind the brain hijack and a few of the 'pieces.' As mentioned in earlier chapters, a "brain hijack" often refers to a situation where the emotional part of the brain, primarily the amygdala, takes over or "hijacks" the rational part of the brain, namely the pre-frontal cortex. This concept is crucial in understanding how we react under stress or emotionally charged situations.

The Amygdala's Role: The amygdala is a part of the limbic system, often associated with emotional processing, especially fear and pleasure. It's like an alarm system for threats, real or perceived, preparing the body for a fight-or-flight response by releasing stress hormones like cortisol and adrenaline. Essentially, this is taking the brain offline momentarily.

Prefrontal Cortex Overridden: The prefrontal cortex is responsible for rational thinking, decision-making, and moderating social behavior. It's the part of the brain that thinks things through and weighs outcomes. During a brain hijack, the amygdala's intense emotional response can override the prefrontal cortex, leading to more emotional than rational reactions.

Fight-or-Flight Response: This evolutionary mechanism primes the body to either fight the threat or flee from it. In modern contexts, this can manifest not just physically but also in emotional responses to non-physical threats, like an argument or a stressful work situation.

Neurotransmitters and Hormones: The process involves a cascade of neurotransmitters and hormones that affect the body's state. For example, cortisol increases glucose in the bloodstream, enhancing the brain's use of glucose and increasing the availability of substances that repair tissues.

Stated another way, imagine your brain is like a car with two drivers: one is the calm, thinking driver who plans the route and makes decisions (the prefrontal cortex), and the other is the quick-reacting driver who hits the gas pedal when they sense danger (the amygdala).

A "brain hijack" is like the quick-reacting driver grabbing the wheel and stepping on the gas without consulting the calm driver. This happens when we're scared or upset, and our body's emergency system kicks in without thinking things through. It's meant to protect us from danger, but sometimes it acts up even when the threat isn't physical, like during a challenging conversation or a stressful moment at work.

After this quick driver takes over, we need time to let the calm driver back in control and slow down the car. At least 90 seconds. That's why we often need time to calm down and think clearly again after getting really upset.

In both scenarios, the essence is that a brain hijack involves an emotional response taking precedence over rational thought, which can lead to impulsive or less-than-ideal reactions to stressful situations.

Overcoming Obstacles and Resilience

Understanding the brain's hijack process is pivotal in recognizing why we react the way we do under stress or when faced with challenges. This automatic response/autopilot default can derail our best intentions (as highlighted in my fraud story), leading to decisions and actions influenced more by immediate emotions than rational thought.

Recognizing this is the first step towards resilience. Resilience isn't just about withstanding pressure; it's about harnessing an awareness of our emotional triggers and automatic responses to navigate them more effectively. By acknowledging the amygdala's role in our emotional reactions, we pave the way for developing strategies that foster a resilient mindset. This mindset enables us to approach obstacles not as insurmountable barriers but as opportunities for growth and learning. As we delve deeper into understanding and building resilience, we equip ourselves with the tools necessary to transform challenges into stepping stones toward personal and professional fulfillment.

Everyday Obstacles

It is pretty clear by now how powerful our brains' natural tendencies affect our everyday lives. The brain is more like an impetuous child ready to lash out in negative behavior because they are not getting their way. The everyday brain just loves to dig up beliefs of negativity or immediate insecurities about ourselves and others. Sometimes, the brain is like a petulant child; no matter what you say, they disagree or find a way to prove you wrong. Each day can be met with unexpected obstacles. Sometimes, each goal and project can inherently bring its own set of obstacles and challenges. I call this the everyday obstacle. You never know when a thought or memory will pop into your mind and trip you up, distracting you from what you were working on. Stop in this immediate moment and ask yourself, how many thoughts are running through your mind at this very moment? Do you notice them?

How many beliefs and conversations are you having in your head about your beliefs? Maybe these conversations are taking place because you are reflecting, or maybe the conversations are taking place because distraction is part of the human challenge we face daily.

When I look back on the situation with my fraud, in the days and weeks following this incident, I often ruminated, and my thoughts would distract me from what I was working on because I kept replaying the scenario and having so much regret. I would snap myself out of this thought loop by repeating the same phrase I tell my clients daily. I'll repeat it throughout this book to see if you pay attention! "QUIT Should'ng All Over Yourself"

Should'ing All Over Yourself

The 'should have' thoughts are NOT productive. They do not serve anything. The more you tell yourself what you could have done, the more you deep-seed the negative thoughts and patterns in your memory.

Our brain's default setting, closely integrated with the amygdala's alert system, naturally prioritizes memories of danger and discomfort. This survival mechanism, crucial for avoiding threats like the instinctual pull away from a hot stove, also biases us towards a fear-centered worldview. While essential for our safety, this tendency can mislead, making us overly fixate on negative experiences. My experience with fraud exemplifies how such a predisposition towards negativity can cloud our judgment, illustrating the brain's default to survival reactions that may not always align with our well-being and can impair our judgment.

When you keep reliving a memory repeatedly and telling yourself what you should have done or could have done, you're reconstructing the memory repeatedly and creating different connections to this memory. Some memories are best left in the past, despite our survival instinct to hold on to every memory.

It's not just what is in the past is in the past. And it's not to negate how you feel. One mistake people make is beating themselves up and trying to move on without fully expressing their feelings. Feelings are good, and feelings are a necessary part of the human experience. In fact, one of the common biases and beliefs that get ingrained in certain people is that feelings are bad, and some people are just too emotional. Guess what? Every thought you think starts with an emotion.

This ingrained focus on the negative profoundly shapes our beliefs and biases, fostering fear and apprehension that can stifle personal growth. Dwelling on past dangers or negative outcomes cultivates a cautious outlook, diminishing our potential. We become emotional about these fears and then feed them with beliefs we have developed, either right or wrong, over time. Fears are just memories that become distorted and project how we view future outcomes. Liberating ourselves from this cycle involves acknowledging and expressing these feelings, then consciously reframing our experiences. This proactive approach not only mitigates the impact of negative biases but also opens up pathways for more positive and empowering beliefs, transforming how we perceive and engage with the world around us.

Every day, obstacles happen to us. Daily minor stresses become big things in your mind. Eventually, small things like a paper cut or a jerk cutting you off in traffic become big in your mind. The accumulation of reactive behavior leads to a stress build-up, turning the mind into a pressure cooker that gets set off with little effort. Making empowered decisions and recognizing the brain hijack is critical to managing and reducing the build-up.

But how? How do we make empowered decisions when triggered, emotional, in the thralls of a situation?

The Thought Loop

Every situation we encounter gets processed through a complex network of our senses. Site, sound, taste, touch, and find
their way to our emotional center. We've talked a great deal
about the amygdala. When we encounter a situation, the brain
processes information through a two-part system involving
emotions and thoughts. Initially, the emotional response is
quick, stemming from the brain's amygdala, which assesses
the emotional significance of the stimulus—whether it's a
threat or reward. Almost simultaneously, the prefrontal cortex, responsible for higher-order thinking, evaluates the situation further, considering past experiences and potential consequences. This dual processing can result in a rapid emotional
reaction rather than a more deliberate, thoughtful response,
shaping our perception and action in any situation.

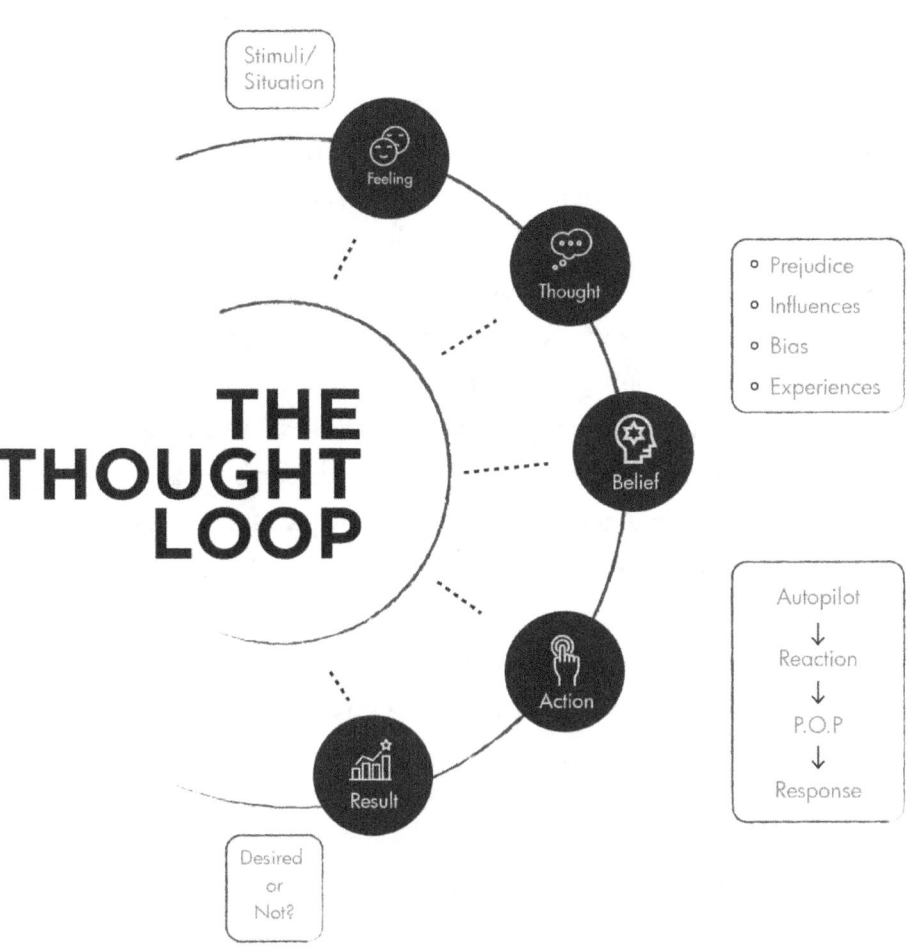

www.heatherjcrider.com

E motions trigger thoughts. Thoughts get influenced or filtered by our experiences, biases, prejudices, and influences. We then make a decision, which is our action. Often, because of our autopilot system, we may act out of hast instead of acting more wisely. Or we act from our default autopilot without thinking, which can be a good thing because it aids us in completing tasks. Imagine how hard it was the first time you drove a car. Learning how to navigate the steering wheel, gear selector, finding the turn signal or the windshield wipers can all be challenging tasks to focus on when you have never done them. Over time, you store this information, and when driving and you need to turn, you just hit the turn signal lever, and now your blinker is on. Your brain is highly efficient and wants to store valuable and useful information to help you think less and do more. In this scenario, the autopilot is a highly efficient and effective system.

But what about when you are emotionally triggered and have to think on the spot? Chances are you are less efficient and might say or do something you don't want to, or you cannot access the information then and might just freeze and say or do nothing.

This is all part of the thought process, what I call the thought loop.

P.O.P

Here is a technique to help you learn how to give yourself space immediately when you may become emotionally triggered and cannot act according to your desires or values.

As you read this, I want you to either slam your hand down on a table or snap your fingers, and simultaneously, I want you to say out loud: POP.

Do it now. Slam your hand down and say out loud. P.O.P.

Now, take a breath.

Take another breath and let your shoulders fall.

Take another breath and let your shoulders fall even more, and this time, ask yourself, what is important now? Simply see what comes to you when you ask this question.

How do you feel? What did you notice?

P.O.P stands for The Power of the Pause.

What this means is that in between stimulus and response lies space. In that space lies your power to choose wisely rather than react hastily, regretfully, or impulsively. To find your power in that space, you must provide the space rather than react immediately.

What this means in real-world speak is to take a break before responding. As stated earlier, typically, 90 seconds is the time you need if your brain is experiencing a brain hijack or even when your brain is experiencing extra stress.

The three breaths technique I illustrated above describes a simple technique to attempt to give your brain time and space. At that time, you were practicing the power of the pause.

Pausing gives you the ability to think clearly. Acting impulsively is sometimes fun, but not every situation allows you the freedom for impulse. The Power of The Pause is one of my secret weapons to invite more peace and calm into my day, moment by moment. This is one of the secret weapons I teach my clients as well. It's simple, and it's extremely effective. I just used it myself.

I wanted you to slap your hand on the table or snap your fingers because if you can create a kinetic and physical connection with your mind and body to remember the power of the pause, you will be more likely to practice it and use it when it matters most.

P.O.P is a perfect acronym to attach to a physical movement that shocks your state into an immediate shift. P.O.P said loudly with a physical act will remind you to practice the P.O.P...the power of the pause.

The more practice and attention we give to our reactions and know that we are in a state of brain hijack, the more we can stop and choose a response we desire. If you look at the thought loop illustration on the prior page, it shows the thought loop and the stages we go through. The question to ask yourself when you reflect upon your decisions is whether the result is a desired one or not. If I get angry at my son and yell at him. My desired outcome is for him to understand my perspective and why I am angry. However, my action, yelling at him, is acting out of anger, and I might say something that harms him, upsets him, or makes him less responsive to listen because of my anger. This is not my desired result, but this is the result I end up with.

You may not think a simple action like snapping your fingers or slapping your hand on the table can snap you back to focus. It's not just a trick; science backs it up.

Washington University School of Medicine's research has shed light on the Somato-Cognitive Action Network (SCAN). This complex network is all about how our physical actions and cognitive processes are deeply connected. It shows us that when we engage in physical actions, like the 'P.O.P' technique, we're not just moving; we're activating parts of our brain to help us shift our focus and attention. This is particularly relevant when we're trying to remember to pause before reacting. It's like creating a mental bookmark that reminds us to take a moment before diving into our usual automatic responses.

But it's not just about neuroscience. The positive psychology field also has much to say about the mind-body connection. Our bodies play a big role in our thinking and feeling, not just carrying out orders from our brains. This is where embodiment theories come into play, suggesting that our physical actions can significantly impact our mental states. So, when we make a conscious effort to 'P.O.P'—that is, trigger the reminder to pause and reflect through a physical action—we're engaging in a practice supported by both neuroscience and psychology. This isn't just a neat trick; it's a way to harness our body's role in shaping our cognitive processes and emotional responses. By understanding this, we can use physical actions like 'P.O.P' as a tool to disrupt the cycle of automatic, often negative, reactions and steer ourselves toward more thoughtful, positive outcomes and desired results.

So, next time you're about to fly off the handle or make a snap decision, attempt to remember the 'P.O.P.' It's not just a quirky thing; it's a science-backed method to help you pause, reflect, and choose a response that aligns more with who you want to be. And the more we practice this, the more we train our brains to focus on the positives and away from the negatives. We're essentially giving our brain a new default setting that's more about thoughtful responses than knee-jerk reactions.

"I get knocked down, but I get up again. You're never gonna keep me down" – Chumbawamba

Doesn't this tune just stick in your head? For me, it does more than that. It speaks to the essence of resilience that resides within each of us. It's a reminder that no matter the adversity we face—personal setbacks, professional challenges, or the internal turmoil of our doubts and fears—we have the innate strength to rise again. Life's obstacles are inevitable, but our response to them defines our path.

The journey of resilience is about recognizing our brain's predisposition towards negativity, a natural survival mechanism that sometimes needs recalibration. It's about choosing to see obstacles not as permanent roadblocks but as opportunities for growth and learning. This choice starts with acknowledging our emotions and the stories we tell ourselves, understanding that we have the power to rewrite these narratives into ones that empower and uplift us.

As we've explored throughout this chapter, transforming our relationship with adversity requires a conscious effort to reshape how we perceive and react to challenges. By acknowledging our feelings and deliberately reframing our experiences, we're not dismissing our emotions but rather choosing to view them through a lens of growth. This process is akin to reshaping the neural pathways in our brain, enabling us to approach future obstacles with wisdom and insight rather than fear.

Drawing on stories of individuals who have lived this mantra, we have endless examples of resilience in action. Consider the entrepreneur who, after facing bankruptcy, used the lessons learned from that failure to build a successful business. Or the athlete who, despite a career-threatening injury, fought through rehabilitation to compete again. Or a single mother of two who has suffered from anxiety and depression used the belief of others to cultivate belief within herself to create a life of her dreams.

These stories are not just tales of overcoming; they are testaments to the human spirit's unyielding capacity for rebounding from setbacks.

Echoing the sentiments of the lyric that I cannot get out of my head, "I get knocked down, but I get up again, you're never gonna keep me down," let us embrace this mantra of resilience. It serves as a beacon, guiding us through life's storms and reminding us that our spirit's capacity to overcome is boundless. Each fall, each setback, is not an end but a step in our journey, a testament to our enduring strength and resilience.

To cultivate this resilient mindset, we begin by embracing our vulnerabilities, allowing ourselves to fully experience the pain of our falls, yet refusing to be defined by them. We shift from seeing ourselves as victims of circumstance to architects of our destiny, understanding that while we cannot control every obstacle life throws our way, we possess the ultimate authority over our reactions.

As we advance towards our goals, remember that true strength lies not in never falling but in our unwavering resolve to rise, time and again, with greater wisdom and determination. The belief in yourself. The belief in your ability to keep moving forward.

In sum, resilience is a practice, a moment-to-moment commitment to confronting our everyday obstacles with mindfulness and courage. Just as life is a series of nows, resilience is the cumulative effect of how we choose to respond to each now. By leaning into calm, making decisions with clarity, and embracing our inner strength, we not only navigate challenges more effectively but also pave the way for a life marked by growth, fulfillment, and an unshakeable sense of empowerment.

Let us move forward with the knowledge that our ability to rise after being knocked down is not just an act of survival but a testament to our capacity for transformation and growth. Ultimately, our resilience carries us through, turning every obstacle into a stepping stone on the path to our greatest potential.

Chapter Summary:

Reflecting on these chapters of my life, I've come to understand the profound strength in vulnerability and courage to believe. Sharing the raw edges of our stories, like the tragic assault on my sister or the overwhelm of new motherhood amidst crisis, does more than recount moments of survival; it unveils the resilience we forge in fire. These experiences, while harrowing, taught me invaluable lessons about the power of human spirit and adaptability. They remind me that even when life's boulders blindside us, our capacity to navigate the rapids, learn from the journey, and emerge with newfound strength is what truly defines us. In embracing our stories, with all their pain and triumph, we find connection, healing, and the courage to face whatever comes next with an open heart, unwavering resilience, and unbreakable belief.

Go Reflect Yourself Reflection Exercise: Obstacles and Resilience

- What immediate insights come up for you from this chapter?

- Reflect on a major obstacle in your life. When you first realized you were in the midst of this obstacle, what were your thoughts and beliefs?

- What were the contributing factors that helped you overcome this obstacle?

- What did you learn from this experience?

- If you faced a similar obstacle today, how could you approach it differently?

- What are you most proud of when reflecting on overcoming this obstacle?

- Repeat the above questions with 2-3 other obstacles you have encountered.

- Who was your hero? When you were little, who did you want to be when you grew up, and why? What did you fantasize about when you were caught in your backyard with no one watching where time stood still? Who did you pretend to be in that moment? What did they possess? What characteristics, what values, what beliefs, with traits, with goals, with dreams, with accomplishments...

- Who are you today? Are you the person you wanted to become? If not, consider where you are today (regardless if you are the person you wanted to become or you are not...) Who you have become today as a combination of your past experiences, your influences, your beliefs or values, and your choices...

- Who you want to be in the future depends upon your current and future experiences, choices, values, beliefs, and decisions.

Chapter Five

From Identity to Excellence and Extraordinariness

"Be more concerned with your character than your reputation because your character is what you really are, while your reputation is merely what others think you are."
~John Wooden

M y entrepreneurial spirit was ignited early in life, start-ing with a flea market in my backyard shed at twelve that failed. This wasn't my first venture; at five, I launched a clothes ironing business on my front porch and a pet-sitting operation at nine. Both businesses closed within a day or two of operation. The pet-sitting endeavor held real promise, though sadly, the market wasn't ready for a nine-year-old pet caretaker. Reflecting on these early initiatives, I realize I was an entrepreneur in the making, years ahead of the burgeoning pet-sitting websites. My most memorable childhood achieve-ment was winning a 'boom box' through a fundraiser earning a spot in the local newspaper.

Looking back to when I was a kid, I can't help but smile about my grandma's unwavering faith in me. No matter what I did, whether failing at my flea market business or winning a contest, she was always there, cheering me on. And it wasn't just about her being a good grandma - she genuinely cared about my big, crazy ideas. She engaged with genuine curiosity and encouragement even when my ideas seemed outlandish, like a five-year-old's ironing service. Her belief wasn't just about celebrating successes; it was about supporting me through failures and changes in direction, reinforcing the idea that belief in oneself is paramount. Her unconditional belief in me fostered an environment where I felt empowered to dream big and take risks.

Throughout her final days, until she passed, it was common for me to bounce ideas off of her, confide in her, talk through my thoughts, change my mind, or move forward with my plans. While she may not have always fully grasped my experiences or ideas, she always believed in my ability to manage them. She encouraged me to explore various possibilities and consider all angles of situations. She nurtured my growth and empowered me to find the tools and resources to overcome obstacles. Her unwavering belief in a brighter future was a true gift, and thanks to her, I, too believe in the power of positivity. And believe in belief! The most important part about her belief was that she believed in me regardless of who I was. Of course, she was proud when I accomplished things and wanted the best for me. She was the first person to push me and always there to challenge me, but because of her belief, I was willing to be pushed and fail.

Fear of failure and judgment is one of the biggest reasons we don't push ourselves to expand beyond our limits. Yet, despite my grandmother's support, a more significant influence loomed that stifled my spirit, a reality I shielded from her.

Growing up, my imagination was as boundless as any child's, filled with dreams of being a superhero. I'd often leap from the couch in my She-ra or Wonderwoman underoos, cloaked in a blanket tied around my neck, pretending to soar through the skies. In these moments, a red blanket became my cape, which was my secret identity. And just between you and me, I sometimes revisit this secret identity, tying a red blanket around my neck, claiming I'm just cold to avoid my kids' teasing.

Another constant in my childhood was shadowing my older sister, my real-life hero, who was everything I aspired to be: beautiful, creative, intelligent, funny, and immensely popular. Our four-year age gap meant I was often just steps behind her, earning us the nickname "Pete and Repeat" from an uncle. She wasn't just my idol; she was my protector in a world that felt uncertain and, at times, turbulent.

As I grew older, I realized just how much of a shield and protector she was for me. My parents, teenagers themselves when they started our family, faced their battles with violence, alcohol abuse, and the myriad challenges of raising two young children in the '70s and '80s. Amidst this chaos, I crafted an illusion of perfection, a shield against the pain and complexity of our reality.

To cope, one of my strategies, in addition to pretending I was a superhero, was to pretend my family was perfect. For some reason, in those years, the topic of divorce had become a confusing topic full of stigma. Divorce is messy and stressful. I've been through one myself, but as a child, I wore the fact that my parents were not divorced as a badge of honor. Despite the apparent struggles and turmoil my family was experiencing, I maintained this facade, never revealing the truth behind my family's closed doors. I never talked with my friends or family about what I witnessed or my challenges at home. I kept them all a secret because I didn't want anyone to know my family was not perfect. When I visited friends' houses and got an inside glimpse of their families and how they operated, the love, laughter, humility, and patience I witnessed with them made me feel even more insecure, envious, and willing to conceal my truth.

One of my friend's father was a well-respected doctor in the area, and when I visited her, I was struck by their tight-knit family and the complete respect I observed among her parents. Another one of my friend's mothers had a very high-profile career, and again, when I would visit them at their house, what I observed was very different from my family dynamics. So, I created in my mind what I wanted my home life to look like, and this was the filter I put in my metaphorical glasses. It was my protective filter to block out any chance someone would see what was happening at home. Little did I know then that people's lives were not always as they seemed; just as I had put on my own set of lenses, sometimes other people did as well.

Everyone struggles at times. Everyone has their insecurities and challenges they would rather not talk about. But in the eyes of a child so focused on the self, you don't realize this.

My parents eventually divorced, and when they did, my rose-colored glasses were crushed. I felt like the entire world I had been protecting to keep a secret was outed and that I had a scarlet letter brightly displayed where everyone knew all my struggles. I felt exposed and ashamed.

My identity became one that I was 'that girl.' What 'that girl' meant, I don't know exactly. I just identified as being the girl from a broken home. My sister had challenges as a teenager and moved out when she was 16. So, my identity was constantly shifting and becoming even more disillusioned by my own glasses.

I was determined to attend college, get a degree, and start my own life. Once out of college, I got a fantastic job with a nice title and salary and started my adult life. My identity became what I did. Then, I struggled to have children, so my identity was once again warped into lack and shame, especially in those stages of life. My womanhood was vulnerable and challenged because I struggled to have children. Eventually, through the magic of modern technology and some miracles, I was able to have two amazing children, so my identity became a mother. Then, as I progressed through life, I had struggles in my marriage and got a divorce. Then, my identity shifted back to one of divorce and devastation. It's interesting how we see ourselves, though, and again, how others view us.

Several years ago, I sat down with a colleague who saw that I had recently released my first book. She said, "I needed to meet with you and figure out what you were doing, or I needed to completely block you from my life because it looks like everything you do turns to gold, and I feel jealous because I want that but don't know how."

WHAT? She thought everything I do turns to gold? How could she believe this? She had no idea about the struggles I was facing at the time. She saw me as accomplished and unaffected by struggles when, at the time, I was a divorced mom of two and enduring a tumultuous business partnership. My business partner was hiding clients and income from me, and I was in a position to need to restart my own business because of this. It was a rocky time for me, yet she had a different perspective. I also had my own identity and how I saw myself. My identity constantly shifted by what I was experiencing in my life, and as I experienced more struggles in my life, my identity continued to shift.

This interaction led me to further self-reflection and exploration, aligning my identity with my values, worth, and integrity to move into a more authentic version of myself.

Identity and Belief

At the core of our being lies the concept of identity, a complex tapestry woven from the threads of our beliefs, experiences, and perceptions. How you view your identity is similar to selecting the right pair of glasses to see the world. Choose the wrong pair, and everything looks blurry; choose the right pair, and suddenly, everything is in crystal clear focus.

Your identity is not just who you think you are—it's the lens through which you see every opportunity, challenge, and possibility. It's the foundation upon which you build your aspirations and achievements. But here's the kicker: what if the glasses you've been wearing all this time are outdated? What if they distort your vision of who you can become?

Let's get real for a moment. We all carry around a mental image of ourselves, a "self-concept," if you will, that's been cobbled together from past experiences, societal labels, and, yes, even those off-hand comments from Aunt Edna over Thanksgiving dinner. This image is as comfortable as an old pair of sneakers, familiar but perhaps a bit too worn to take us where we want to go. The question is, are you ready to trade in those sneakers for something that can truly take you the distance?

Understanding this interplay between belief and identity is crucial for anyone seeking to navigate the journey of personal growth and transformation.

Imagine for a moment you're a high performer, sophisticated, always looking for growth, more money, and more peace. You've got goals, aspirations, and a burning desire to achieve excellence. But here's the rub: your current self-perceptions are like a bungee cord tied around your waist, pulling you back just as you're about to leap. The truth is, the gap between where you are and where you want to be is bridged by your identity—how you see yourself in the mirror of your mind.

Beliefs act as the lens through which we view reality, coloring our experiences and dictating our responses. They are the architects of our reality, constructing the boundaries of what we perceive to be possible. Our identity, in turn, is built upon these beliefs, becoming a reflection of what we believe to be true about ourselves. Maxwell Maltz pioneered this understanding in his work on self-image, where he posited that our self-image fundamentally determines our capacity to achieve success and fulfillment. If you look around and realize you want to change your external circumstances (career, relationships, financial state); in that case, the way you see yourself and how you approach life starts with your internal state—your beliefs and identity.

To transform our lives, we must first delve into the depths of our beliefs, questioning and challenging the ones that limit us. It is within this introspection that we discover the power to redefine our identity. This process is not about discarding who we are but shedding the layers that no longer serve us, revealing a more authentic and empowered self. As we align our beliefs with our aspirations, our identity begins to shift, moving us closer to the realization of our true potential.

Picture two climbers, Alex and Jordan, both aiming to conquer the same daunting peak. Alex sees himself as an amateur, cautious, and unsure, while Jordan views herself as a master climber, confident and prepared. They both face the same challenges and treacherous paths, but who do you think reaches the summit? Jordan, of course! Not because the mountain was any less dangerous on her path but because her identity as a master climber shaped her approach to every obstacle.

This is where the wisdom of Maxwell Maltz comes in, reminding us that our self-image sets the boundaries of what we believe is possible. It's not just about setting goals; it's about aligning them with an identity that empowers us to achieve them. Think of it as upgrading your mental operating system to match the ambitions you've set for yourself.

Yet, it's crucial to recognize that our journey toward excellence is often paved not just with triumphs but also with failures. These setbacks, while disheartening at the moment, are not detours but integral parts of the path itself. They offer unparalleled opportunities for learning and self-discovery, challenging us to reassess our beliefs and identity. As I have reflected on various parts and situations in my life and my failures, I spent years 'shoulding' all over myself with regret. I now reframe my thoughts when I go down the 'shame, blame, regret, guilt' path. Instead of being stuck on this path, I remind myself that my failures are truly what has made me me. Failure teaches us resilience, humility, and the courage to confront our limitations, inviting us to redefine our self-image not as fixed and immutable but as adaptable and evolving. Embracing failure as a catalyst for growth enables us to approach each obstacle not with trepidation but with a curiosity that fuels our ascent toward our peak potential.

Bridging The Gap

So, how do we bridge the gap? How do we reshape our identity to pave the way for excellence and extraordinariness?

Laugh Out Loud

As we embark on the task of bridging the gap between our present identity and the extraordinary heights we aim to reach; it's crucial to harness the power of humor as a companion on this journey. Humor offers us a unique lens through which to view our challenges, lightening the weight of our struggles and unveiling the absurdity in our setbacks. My journey has taught me that laughter, albeit sometimes misused as a defense mechanism during moments of cognitive overload, is a testament to the resilience of the human spirit. While it may sometimes confuse those around me in social situations, I cherish my propensity to find laughter in the face of adversity. It allows me to perceive situations laden with irony and serendipity, transforming potential fuel for anger or deep sadness into opportunities for healing and growth. Recognizing that moments devoid of laughter signal a need for introspection has been a pivotal realization in my path. Once I realized I could laugh at my past rather than run from it, I found the levity healing. I realized that looking at what I endured as humorous and pulling the specific humorous undertones helped me remove some of the clouds I carried.

By weaving humor into our process of self-reflection and goal setting, we not only make the journey toward excellence more enjoyable but also cultivate a mindset that doesn't dwell too heavily on our failures or take ourselves too seriously. This light-hearted approach has the power to transform our perception of obstacles, converting seemingly insurmountable barriers into manageable hurdles.

I recall a time when a project I was deeply invested in fell through. Instead of succumbing to frustration, I laughed at the unfortunate events that led to its demise. This shift in perspective didn't just help me cope—it opened up new avenues for creative thinking and problem-solving that I hadn't considered before.

As you sift through the narrative of your own story and evaluate the beliefs that have sculpted your identity, grant yourself the grace to chuckle at the slip-ups encountered along the way. Embracing this levity is not merely a mechanism for coping; it's a strategic tool that fortifies resilience, fosters openness, and enhances adaptability, ensuring that our quest for excellence is imbued with joy and purpose. Laughing at ourselves, taking life's curveballs with a pinch of humor, signals to others—and more importantly, to ourselves—that we are open to embracing life's experiences, not as personal insults, but as universal episodes of the human condition. In this journey from identity to excellence, integrating humor into our toolkit not only lightens our load but also shapes the very essence of our being, proving that the gap between current self-perceptions and the pursuit of excellence is bridged by the laughter that echoes through our most trying times. How do you see yourself now?

Identifying The Gap

First, question the narrative. Every belief you have about yourself was written in the storybook of your life by someone—parents, teachers, friends, and yes, even Aunt Edna. It's time to become the editor of your own story. Which beliefs serve your journey to excellence, and which are holding you back?

Next, visualize the identity you need to achieve your goals. If you want to earn more, what qualities does a high earner possess? Confidence? Savvy? Unwavering determination? Start embodying those qualities now, even if it feels like you're just playing a role at first.

Remember, in the theatre of your mind, you're the star of the show. And also remember humor. One tool I use for myself and my clients is the visualization imagination, which can work in many scenarios. First, infuse humor into the visualizations. There is a psychological trick to bringing levity into situations by creating a visual in your mind of a situation that is outlandish rather than serious. For example, when my former spouse would say something offensive to me, instead of looking at him with anger and feeling like a victim, I would pretend his head inflated and he became a hot air balloon. I envisioned his voice becoming higher pitched as his head expanded. The higher his voice became, his head would begin to detach from his body, eventually quickly whizzing by making funny noises out loud like a whoopie cushion. Can you imagine something similar? This visualization has become one of my go-to coping visualizations when I feel triggered.

Let's expand on humor as a tool.

The psychological trick I referred to uses humor to reframe a challenging or negative situation, reducing its emotional impact and changing your reaction. By imagining something outlandish or absurd, like a former spouse's head inflating and turning him into a hot air balloon during a conflict, you shift the perspective from anger or victimhood to humor and detachment. This strategy is a form of cognitive reappraisal, a psychological technique that involves changing how you think about a situation to change your emotional response.

The Science Behind Humorous Visualization

Cognitive reappraisal is a core component of emotional regulation strategies as outlined in psychological research, including the work of James Gross, a professor of psychology at Stanford University. We can change an emotional impact by altering the meaning of a situation that elicits an emotional response. Humorous visualization acts as a form of cognitive reappraisal by transforming a situation's perceived threat or negativity into something absurd and non-threatening.

Imagining a humorous or outlandish outcome creates psychological distance from the situation. This distancing helps reduce immediate emotional responses such as anger or hurt, allowing for a more measured and calm reaction. It's similar to techniques used in mindfulness and meditation, where observation without emotional engagement is encouraged to foster emotional balance.

Neurological Impact: Humor and laughter trigger the release of endorphins, the body's natural feel-good chemicals. They also reduce the levels of stress hormones, which can help lower anxiety and tension. The act of laughing or even just finding something amusing can create a positive emotional state, counteracting the negative emotions associated with the stressful situation.

Levity and humor have been shown to enhance creativity and flexibility in thinking. Viewing a situation through a humorous lens makes you more likely to see alternative solutions and perspectives. This cognitive flexibility can be especially beneficial in interpersonal conflicts where rigid thinking can escalate tensions.

Practical Application

To apply this technique, pause and intentionally conjure an exaggeratedly humorous or absurd image related to the trigger when confronted with a situation that might elicit a negative emotional response. The key is to make the visualization vivid and engaging enough to elicit a genuine emotional shift from stress or anger to amusement or neutrality.

Using humorous visualization as a form of cognitive reappraisal is a powerful tool for emotional regulation. It leverages the brain's ability to reinterpret situations, the psychological benefits of humor, and the body's physiological response to laughter to transform how we experience and respond to potential stressors. This strategy helps manage emotional responses in the moment and, over time, can contribute to a more resilient and adaptive emotional landscape.

The final way to incorporate visualization is to set your goals with your new identity in mind. These aren't just any goals; they're milestones on becoming the version of yourself that can achieve extraordinariness.

Each goal achieved confirms your evolving identity, a reinforcement that you are indeed becoming who you aspire to be.

This journey from identity to excellence is not a solemn march. It's a dance, a playful experiment in becoming more of who you really are and tapping into the superpowers you already possess, nurturing them to aid you in achieving your desired goals. So, as you embark on this path, keep a light heart and a keen sense of humor. After all, pursuing excellence and extraordinariness is not just about the destination; it's about who you become along the way.

The identity you adopt shapes the life you lead. Viewing your identity as a malleable masterpiece opens the door to endless possibilities. It's time to put on your new pair of glasses, lace up those upgraded sneakers, and start the journey from where you are to where you have the potential to be. The gap between current self-perceptions and the pursuit of excellence is only as wide as you believe it to be. So, how do you see yourself now, and what are you accountable for?

Embracing Your Unique Narrative

How often do we dismiss our life as unworthy of a story? We look up to figures like Michael Jordan, Lady Gaga, Sandra Bullock, and other luminaries, marveling at the tales of their triumphs and trials, thinking our own experiences somehow fall short. Yet, this perspective overlooks a fundamental truth: we all possess a tapestry of unique, crazy, wonderful events that have shaped us.

In the grand scheme of life, we find ourselves at a crossroads of uniqueness and universality. Each event that has unfolded in our lives is uniquely ours, painting a distinct portrait of who we are. However, beneath these individual stories lies the bedrock of the human experience—a shared journey of heartaches, losses, ups and downs, and victories. This duality doesn't diminish our stories; it elevates them, reminding us that while the specifics of our narratives may differ, the essence of what it means to be human is shared.

It's easy to believe that our lives aren't as compelling as those who stand in the spotlight, that our challenges and victories aren't as noteworthy. But every person has stories brimming with lessons, emotions, and insights. The fabric of our life, woven from moments of joy, sorrow, failure, and success, is inherently story-worthy because it is uniquely ours and yet deeply connected to the collective human saga.

Moving Into Excellence by Owning Your Story

To enter a space of excellence and extraordinariness, we must first own our stories with pride and acceptance. Embracing your uniqueness and identity, with all its quirks, strengths, and vulnerabilities, is the first step towards liberating yourself from the chains of conformity and mediocrity. It's about celebrating who you are and, equally important, who you are not.

Being extraordinary isn't about transcending your story or becoming someone else; it's about fully inhabiting your story and extracting the wisdom it holds. The road to excellence is paved with the stones of your unique experiences, and it's by walking this road with authenticity and courage you begin to shed the weight of limiting beliefs.

Limiting beliefs are barriers to our growth, convincing us that we are less capable, less worthy, or less interesting than we truly are. By confronting and moving past these beliefs, we open ourselves to the fullness of our potential. This process isn't about erasing our past or discarding our essence but about reinterpreting our narrative to empower and uplift us.

Be Free to Be You

At its heart, the journey to becoming extraordinary is a journey of liberation—freedom from the constraints of past definitions of success, freedom from the fear of judgment, and freedom to express and accept oneself fully. This liberation doesn't mean you won't face doubts or challenges, but it equips you with the resilience and self-belief to navigate them.

As you stand at the precipice of change, looking towards the horizon of your potential, remember that the power to bridge the gap between your current self and your extraordinary future self lies in the stories you choose to tell yourself. Embrace your narrative, cherish your uniqueness, and step forward with the knowledge that your journey, with all its intricacies, is not just worthy of a story—it is the story.

Ultimately, moving into excellence and embracing extraordinariness is a deeply personal yet universally shared journey. It's about owning your story, breaking free from limiting beliefs, and stepping into a future where you are not just existing but thriving in your authenticity. Let your unique narrative be the wings that propel you toward your extraordinary destiny.

Go Reflect Yourself Reflection Exercise: Identity to Extraordinary

1. Who Are You Beyond Your Roles?
- Reflect on who you are beyond the roles you play in daily life (e.g., parent, partner, professional). What intrinsic qualities or values define you?

2. What Is Your Identity?
- How would you describe your identity in terms of your beliefs, values, and the aspirations that drive you? How does this identity align with the person you wish to become?

3. How Have Your Experiences Shaped Your Identity?
- Consider the experiences that have significantly impacted shaping your identity. How have these moments influenced your beliefs about yourself and the world?

4. What Aspects of Your Identity Are You Proud Of?

- Identify the aspects of your identity that fill you with pride. How do these elements reflect your core values and achievements?

5. Where Do You Feel a Gap in Your Identity?

- Where do you perceive a gap between your current self-perceptions and the person you aspire to be? What steps can you take to bridge this gap?

6. How Do Limiting Beliefs Affect Your Identity?

- Reflect on any limiting beliefs that might be holding you back from fully embracing your desired identity. How can you challenge and transform these beliefs?

7. In What Ways Can You Use Humor to Explore Your Identity?

- Consider how humor can be a tool for exploring and expressing your identity. Have there been moments when laughter helped you overcome challenges or see yourself in a new light?

8. How Does Your Identity Influence Your Goals?

- Think about the goals you have set for yourself. How do these goals reflect your identity, and how might aligning your goals more closely with your identity enhance your journey toward excellence?

9. What Changes Would You Like to Make to Your Identity?

- Envision how adopting these changes could impact your path to personal and professional fulfillment.

10. How Will You Live Out Your Identity Going Forward? - Looking ahead, how do you plan to live out your identity in a way that feels authentic and fulfilling? What actions will you take to embody the qualities and values that are important to you?

How does the idea of my identity being a "malleable master-piece" inspire me to approach personal growth differently?

What practical steps can I take to begin embodying the empowering beliefs I wish to adopt?

How will changing my internal narrative to align with my desired identity affect my pursuit of excellence and personal fulfillment?

Common Limiting Beliefs and Empowering Alternatives

Limiting Belief: I'm not good enough to achieve my dreams.
- Empowering Belief: I have unique strengths and talents that can propel me towards my dreams.

Limiting Belief: Mistakes are failures.
- Empowering Belief: Every mistake is a learning opportunity that brings me closer to my goals.

Limiting Belief: I must do everything perfectly.
- Empowering Belief: Progress is more important than perfection. Every step forward counts.

Limiting Belief: It's too late to change my path.
- Empowering Belief: It's never too late to pursue a new direction or passion in life.

Limiting Belief: I don't have what it takes to be successful.
- Empowering Belief: Success is built on effort and learning, and I am fully capable of both.

Limiting Belief: I'm not as talented as others.
- Empowering Belief: My journey is unique, and comparing it to others doesn't define my worth or potential.

Limiting Belief: I can't make a significant impact.

- Empowering Belief: Small changes and actions can lead to a significant impact over time.

Limiting Belief: If I fail, people will judge me.

- Empowering Belief: My worth isn't determined by others' opinions. Courage to try is what truly matters.

Limiting Belief: I must meet everyone's expectations.

- Empowering Belief: Living authentically according to my values and aspirations is most fulfilling.

Limiting Belief: Change is too hard.

- Empowering Belief: Change is a process that happens one step at a time, and I am capable of navigating it.

Chapter Six

Earning Yourself - Self-Integrity

"Never settle for anything less than what you deserve, it's not pride, it's self-respect." ~Chanakya

Growing up, my family often gathered for parties, summer BBQs, and reunions. As the youngest grandchild in a huge family, I naturally became more of an observer and follower. With over 20 first cousins, all older than me, I had no choice.

One summer afternoon, a large group of older kids were at my grandmother's house when one of my aunts announced she wanted to take everyone to Dairy Queen for ice cream. One of my closest cousins, who is only eleven months older than me, said she wanted to stay back and wait for the snow cone truck to come by, asking me to stay with her. I really wanted the ice cream. You might assume that because my father worked in an ice cream factory, I would have been sick of ice cream by then. But in reality, Dairy Queen was a rare treat I seldom enjoyed, precisely because my father worked at the ice cream factory!

The moment of decision arrived: my aunt urged, "Hurry up, Heather, are you coming with us or not?" Simultaneously, my cousin pleaded for me to stay with her, as no one else would. I reluctantly agreed to stay back for the snow cone truck. My disappointment was palpable when my other cousins returned, flaunting their delicious Blizzards and chocolate-dipped ice cream cones. I was mad at myself for letting my cousin sway me when, deep down, I had yearned for that ice cream.

This might seem trivial to some—I still got a snow cone. But the crux of my disappointment lay not in the treat I received but in realizing that I had ignored my desires to accommodate someone else's. This episode from over 35 years ago remains vivid in my memory. I've recounted this story countless times, using it as a metaphor during my coaching sessions: "Choose the ice cream!"

What I felt that day wasn't about the ice cream or the snow cone; it was about the disappointment in not choosing what I truly wanted. I struggled with the decision, then scolded myself upon seeing everyone else enjoying their ice cream, feeling left out by my own doing. I didn't blame my cousin for her request; she pursued what she wanted. My real lesson was recognizing that I hadn't advocated for my desires.

Such moments, where we allow others' wishes to override our own, can lead to a cascade of regret, guilt, and shame, undermining our self-integrity. Of course, there are times when we decide in favor of others, which is part of life's give and take.

However, it's crucial to discern when these decisions are at the expense of our self-respect and integrity.

This seemingly small moment of choice illuminates a more profound truth about honoring our desires. It highlights the importance of listening to our inner voice and standing firm in our choices, a lesson in self-integrity that, though simple, has profound implications for living authentically and fulfilling our true desires.

The Path to Self-Integrity

Knowing Your Values: The Compass of Your Soul

First and foremost, let's dive into the essence of what makes you, you—your values. These aren't just preferences or likes; they're the core principles guiding your existence. Finding and choosing your values isn't about adopting what looks good on paper or what society applauds. It's about peering into the depths of your soul and acknowledging what truly resonates with your essence. We've covered in earlier chapters how your beliefs are formed and shaped by outside influences. Values are formed the same way, typically how we are influenced. When you examine your values and live within them, you are living in alignment with who you are.

How to Discover Your Values?

Start by reflecting on moments when you felt passionate about life, where you felt most alive and most yourself. What were you doing? Who were you with? What principles were you up-holding? These instances are your clues. If honesty lights you up, then integrity is your beacon. If helping others gives you purpose, then service is your guide. Remember, discovering your values isn't an overnight task. It's a journey of self-explo-ration. Sit with yourself, ask the hard questions, and listen to the whispers of your heart. Your values are there, waiting to be acknowledged and embraced.

Knowing your values is one thing, but living them—that's where the true challenge lies. It's easy to say you value some-thing, but actions are the accurate measure of integrity. This is where you prove your worth, not to the world, but to the most critical audience—yourself.

Every day, life presents you with choices. The small ones, like whether to wake up early for that morning run. And the big ones, like standing up for what's right, even when difficult. Each choice is an opportunity to align with your values.

Let's say you value health, yet you consistently choose con-venience over nutrition or laziness over activity. There's a mis-alignment there, a gap between who you say you are and who you're being. Closing that gap is about making choices that reflect your values, even when it's hard, especially when it's hard.

If you value discipline, set a goal, wake up at 5 AM daily, and stick to it. Prove to yourself that you can commit and follow through.

If integrity is your cornerstone, then be your word. If you say you'll do something, do it. This builds self-trust and proves your worth to the most critical judge—yourself.

The essence of self-integrity lies not just in the grand gestures we make before the world but in the quiet promises we keep to ourselves. It's in the seemingly minor decisions, like choosing between ice cream and a snow cone, where our true values are tested and our character is shaped. Self-integrity is the bedrock upon which personal development and leadership are built, serving as a compass that guides us toward our true north.

Neuroscience and Self-Integrity

In the realm of neuroscience, the concept of self-integrity can be linked to the idea of cognitive dissonance—the psychological discomfort experienced when our actions are not aligned with our beliefs and values. The brain seeks harmony between these elements, and when they are misaligned, it triggers a stress response, signaling that something is amiss. This stress can be alleviated through actions that realign our behavior with our values, restoring a sense of integrity.

For instance, consider the process of goal-setting. Neuroscience reveals that setting and achieving goals not only provides a sense of accomplishment but also strengthens neural pathways associated with self-efficacy and motivation. When we set a goal, the brain's reward system is activated, releasing dopamine—a neurotransmitter linked to pleasure and motivation. This biochemical response rewards the pursuit of goals and reinforces the behavior, leading to goal achievement.

On the flip side of the goal, the coin comes when our goals consistently fall short. Facing the disappointment of not meeting our goals, especially personal ones, stirs a deep sense of dissatisfaction.

Take the common resolution of working out seven days a week—a goal set with the best intentions, albeit lofty. Yet, when life intervenes, and we find ourselves only hitting the gym once a week, the recurring failure doesn't just disappoint; it starts chipping away at our self-integrity. Proving to ourselves each time we 'skip the gym' that we cannot reach our goals. This repeated pattern makes us feel lousy, not because of the missed workouts but because each lapse reminds us of our inability to keep a promise to ourselves. In this instance, it's not about failing others; it's the realization that what we tell ourselves we will do, we don't, and then we can't trust ourselves to honor our intentions.

The real sting comes from the self-perpetuating belief that we are not worthy, a conclusion drawn from our continuous failure to live up to our own expectations. Setting a goal as ambitious as working out daily without accounting for life's unpredictability sets us up for failure. More critically, it reinforces a damaging narrative six days a week—that we lack the discipline or willpower to follow through on our word.

However, when encountering consistent challenges, self-doubt, and an overall sense of 'beat yourself up-itis,' sometimes you must do more self-reflection and go beyond values; you must dig deep into your responsibility for your actions and take accountability.

Recognizing the sting of disappointment in ourselves for not living up to our expectations is a crucial step toward self-awareness. It's a moment that calls for reflection and a transformation in how we respond to our shortcomings. So often, we find ourselves trapped in a cycle of self-blame and regret, which only deepens our sense of failure. Yet, at this juncture, an opportunity for profound change emerges. The journey from self-reproach to self-empowerment begins with a shift in perspective—from viewing our failures as endpoints to seeing them as catalysts for growth. This is where the concept of radical responsibility comes into play. It's about moving beyond the surface level of our actions and delving into the deeper currents that drive our behavior. It's about taking ownership of our lives in a way that transcends the immediate pain of unmet goals and opens us up to the transformative power of true self-integrity."

Radical Responsibility

Throughout much of my life, I grappled with feelings that eerily resembled a mid-life crisis, striking as early as my twenties. Fresh out of college embarking on my first corporate job, I was caught in a tumultuous mix of boredom and self-doubt. This period was particularly confusing for me; I had just achieved a significant milestone - becoming the first in my family to graduate from college. Yet, the anticipated satisfaction eluded me, leaving me to wonder: How could I feel so unfulfilled?

Looking back on the wisdom I've since gathered, I understand that these feelings stemmed mainly from my relationship with self-integrity and the promises I'd made to myself. As my journey unfolded, what was highlighted was the pivotal role that making and keeping promises to oneself plays in nurturing personal development and crafting a life infused with purpose and meaning.

Self-Reflection and Personal Responsibility

It was a cool, damp morning as I walked through the woods on my property. I often strolled down this path, surrounded by the loud rustling of leaves, a symphony played by squirrels and other woodland creatures. Sometimes, I wondered if I might stumble upon a giant deer or be startled by some large animal. More often than not, it was just bunnies, squirrels, and birds. I never ventured too far, fearing I might get lost, but I allowed myself to wander wherever my feet would take me, trusting in my sense of direction and the belief that the path would lead me right.

Consumed with my thoughts, it was hard to fully immerse myself in the true beauty and nature surrounding me. I was fortunate to have this property and walk these paths whenever possible. At the time, however, I didn't fully appreciate my fortune. These walks became my solace, a place where I could be alone, which I loved. Yet, they also became a space where my thoughts overpowered me, trying to process the events of my life. My mind often wandered to questions like, "Why am I so depressed? What is missing in my life? Why can't I be happy?" They seemed like simple questions, but they were confusing and overwhelming. I had a 'good' life without any significant wants or needs. I wasn't a millionaire, nor did I have an excess of money in the bank, but all my basic needs were met. Still, I felt stressed, anxious, and deeply unhappy.

I had believed that achieving certain milestones – career success and financial stability – would automatically lead to happiness. But, to my dismay, they did not. What I didn't realize at the time was that I was asking myself the wrong questions. I was fixated on what was wrong and why I was miserable. Questions like, "Why did my spouse, at the time, behave this way or not understand me? Why was my former mother-in-law so intrusive? Why couldn't my boss see her insensitivity? Why were my clients so emotional?"

You see, I was framing questions that cast me as the victim. I reveled in being the victim, comparing my life and emotions to everyone else's. My family had disappointed me growing up, and I had experienced a lot of anger, violence, and abuse. Because I didn't want to face the truth, I had to finally take radical responsibility for my emotions, decisions, and life.

Let's delve into the realm of radical responsibility. Don't let the term 'radical' startle you. It's not about joining a revolution, unless that revolution is within yourself! This journey is about introspection and understanding the chasm between who we are and aspire to be. It's about the dreams we've nurtured, the achievements we've celebrated, and the aspirations that slipped through our fingers. It's a journey that requires both introspection and faith – faith in ourselves and the belief that we can bridge this gap.

Imagine standing at the edge of a canyon. On one side is your current self, laden with experiences and lessons. Across the gap is the person you yearn to become, adorned with the habits and traits you admire. Bridging this gap requires more than a leap of faith; it demands radical responsibility and a steadfast belief in your potential.

Self-reflection can be intimidating. It feels like confronting your shortcomings, like looking into a mirror that reveals not just your face but the contours of your soul. It's challenging work, but it's the kind that leads to transformation. This was the very thing I resisted. My walks in the woods weren't about self-reflection but wallowing in self-pity and reinforcing my belief that I was a victim. These walks reinforced my position in the 'most crappy things that have happened to me' race. But who was I racing? Who was I competing against? Why was it a competition of who was more pitiful? What did that prove?

My journey could have been smoother. I've seen highs and lows, built businesses, and watched them crumble. Had relationships that ended. At one point, I lost everything. It was easy to play the blame game – the business partner, the circumstances, even my parents and past relationships. I was a maestro conducting an orchestra of excuses.

But here's the crux: the only thing we truly control is our thoughts and actions. When I began unpacking my life, I realized I had to take responsibility for my part. This wasn't about self-blame; it was about empowerment. It was about owning my thoughts, beliefs, actions, and, consequently, the results.

Of course, external influences do exist, but we hold the reins of our responses.

This might sound intense, but it's essentially about taking a hard, honest look at ourselves – our past, our aspirations, and, importantly, the gap between the two. It's about recognizing the dreams we've chased, the milestones we've achieved, and the goals that still elude us. It's about having the faith to confront hard truths about ourselves to believe in our capacity for growth and self-improvement, leading to accomplishment and absolute fulfillment.

Now, let's ponder a challenging question: What is the state of your life? Financially, relationally, physically – if something's amiss, there's a reason. If your go-to response is an excuse, it's time to reevaluate. Excuses are like comfort food – momentarily satisfying but ultimately unfulfilling. I've eaten enough comfort food to know this firsthand!

Taking radical responsibility is about courage – the courage to face ourselves in the mirror and see not just the flaws but the potential for growth, love, and light. It's about acknowledging our role in our current state, not with self-criticism, but with kindness and a resolve to improve. It's about having the faith to believe that we can change and that we can be better.

But hang on a minute. How do we face ourselves in the mirror and get rid of that pesky little negative voice nagging at us? Well, my friend, that voice is no friend to you because it's usually the ego talking.

Ego keeps that self-pity party going like an uninvited guest who won't leave. It feels good sometimes, like a warm blanket of pity and excuses. It's like a mischievous pet, sometimes taking control when we least expect it. Embracing radical responsibility means kicking out this uninvited guest or training this pet, acknowledging its presence but not letting it lead the way. It's about having the belief in ourselves to make this change.

But wait a second. What about the brain?

I mentioned one of my rough patches in life. My brain, particularly my amygdala, was in overdrive during this period. When I talked about my walks in the woods, I didn't calm my amygdala. Instead, I fueled its overactive nature. As described in earlier chapters, the amygdala is a key player in our brain's limbic system and is crucial for processing emotions, especially fear and pleasure. [1]

When we face stress or disappointment, the amygdala can hijack our rational thinking, leading to impulsive decisions or overwhelming emotions. Recognizing this can help us understand why we react the way we do under stress.

When stressed or anxious, it can trigger a cascade of reactions, often leading us to react impulsively or feel overwhelmed. This is a natural response, but understanding it can help us manage these reactions better. At that time in my life, I did not understand any of my emotions. I felt like something was wrong with me, but instead of reflecting, I kept the blame train running hard on its tracks.

Taking radical responsibility meant I had to look beyond external circumstances and examine my role in my own life. It was about acknowledging that while I couldn't control everything, I had the power to shape my responses and decisions. Even though I didn't really want to, it was more familiar and comfortable to remain in the blame game than to accept my involvement in my current circumstances. Once I realized my thoughts could change, and all along, I had the power to change my brain. This realization is deeply rooted in the concept of neuroplasticity – our brain's ability to rewire and adapt based on our experiences and actions. [2]

---

1. https://pubmed.ncbi.nlm.nih.gov/34072960/

2. https://www.ncbi.nlm.nih.gov/pmc/articles/PMC4026979/

As we reflect on our lives, it's crucial to recognize the role of the prefrontal cortex, the brain's executive center. This area is responsible for decision-making, planning, and moderating social behavior. When we engage in self-reflection, we're essentially activating this part of our brain, encouraging it to assess our past actions and plan future ones. It's like a seasoned captain steering the ship of our thoughts through turbulent waters.

The prefrontal cortex is one of the last brain regions to fully mature, often reaching full development in the mid-20s.[3] This prolonged development period may explain why decision-making and impulse control continue to evolve into early adulthood. Furthermore, the PFC is capable of neuroplasticity, meaning it can change and adapt based on experiences, which is crucial for learning and adapting behavior over time.

Taking radical responsibility involves a dance between the prefrontal cortex and the amygdala. It's about calming the emotional storms of the amygdala through mindful reflection, allowing the prefrontal cortex to regain control and guide us toward more rational, considered decisions. It's about having faith in our brain's ability to adapt and change, to believe in the power of neuroplasticity. To believe in the power of ourselves!

Neuroplasticity plays a vital role in this process. This remarkable ability of our brain to change and adapt in response to experience means that each act of radical responsibility rewires our brain, strengthening pathways associated with self-awareness, emotional regulation, and resilience. Each

---

3. https://www.ncbi.nlm.nih.gov/pmc/articles/PMC2892678/

time we confront a challenge or acknowledge our role in a situation, we're not just making a psychological shift but physically reshaping our brains.

As we engage with self-reflection, we're doing more than introspection; we're participating in a neural exercise. It's like exercising a muscle – the more we practice, the stronger and more resilient we become. Approaching self-reflection with a relaxed mind is crucial because stress can activate the brain's fight-or-flight response, hindering our ability to think clearly. By calming our minds, we create an optimal environment for the prefrontal cortex to process information effectively. You can transform not just your mindset but also your brain's functioning. It's about leveraging your understanding of the brain to foster personal growth and resilience.

Understanding the neuroscience behind our actions and reactions empowers us to take radical responsibility not just as a philosophical concept but as a tangible, brain-based practice. It's about harnessing the power of our brain's plasticity to mold ourselves into the individuals we aspire to be. It's about having the belief and faith in ourselves to foster personal growth and resilience.

In my journey, I had to confront that I was often my biggest obstacle. Blaming others – be it business partners, clients, life circumstances, or even my upbringing – was a way to avoid facing my contributions to my situation. This isn't about self-blame; it's about empowerment. By acknowledging our role, we take back control and open the door to meaningful change.

Recognizing my role in my own life was a pivotal moment of growth and empowerment. It's a realization that's not unique to me but shared by many who have faced similar crossroads. A prime example of this is the story of my client, Steve, whose journey from high achievement to overwhelming burnout underscores the universal challenge of aligning our actions with our deepest values and responsibilities."

What About Steve

Steve, a client referred to me a few years back, was a super high achiever. He was an athlete in his teens and twenties and owned a successful, booming business. He came to me experiencing extreme stress and burnout. Overwhelmed and frustrated, he didn't label his experience as burnout but displayed all the classic symptoms. His relationship was suffering, and his thriving business had become an overwhelming challenge.

After several neuroperformance coaching sessions, we uncovered a specific pattern Steve was encountering. His brain exhibited all the classic signs of stress loop burnout, and he lacked techniques to mitigate these symptoms. Initially, he was closed-minded, too consumed by his patterns and how his aversions affected him. He was angry, causing self-inflicted harm to his business, relationships, and happiness.

Steve was accustomed to ultra-competitive environments where struggle and conflict were seen as motivators for achieving more, and years of functioning this way led him to constant competition with others and himself.

While this mentality can be helpful in some situations to push through challenges, over time, it can lead to self-loathing and resentment towards everything around oneself – as Steve put it.

The biggest obstacle Steve had to confront was himself. He took no responsibility for his approach or behaviors. His win-at-all-costs attitude was backfiring, and he was losing in life. He had lost belief in himself, feeling that he wasn't as valuable to his family or employees if he didn't achieve more. His constant competition pushed away the things and people who mattered most to him.

Once we developed his awareness, Steve opened up to the journey of radical responsibility, self-reflection, and belief in his ability to change his circumstances. He had to own that his current dilemma resulted from years of habits and beliefs.

Taking radical responsibility is about owning where you are now, who you are, and what you need to overcome to get to where and who you want to be.

In Steve's case, he first had to forgive himself and take responsibility for his mindset. He suffered from the 'not good enough' syndrome, thinking chasing the next big thing would bring happiness. But once he realized he was always chasing, he began to see things differently.

We started small with simple daily responsibility reflections. Steve developed tools to combat his stress, enabling him to reflect on his beliefs and behaviors. By catching his thoughts during the day, he could counterbalance them with productive action instead of reactive patterns.

His radical responsibility meant being honest with himself about his thoughts. For many years, he had tormented himself with thoughts that led him to struggle more, beating himself up if he wasn't working 14 hours a day or constantly developing new ideas.

The transformation didn't happen overnight, but there were significant shifts over time. He realized he was bored with his life because he lived on autopilot. He soon sold his business and started a new one that fueled his true passion. He developed habits that focused on himself and maintaining a healthy mind. His relationships flourished with open and honest communication. Most importantly, he felt healthier and more at peace.

This experience taught him the power of taking ownership of his actions and beliefs. It showed him that when we stop blaming and start believing in ourselves, we unlock the potential to change not just our circumstances but our entire life's trajectory. In Steve's case, his vulnerability to himself and others was critical. He dared to be honest with himself, which led him to feel better, look better, and truly enjoy life for the first time because now, he was free!

Steve's journey vividly illustrates the transformative power of taking radical responsibility for one's own life. His story demonstrates that when we cease the blame game and start cultivating belief in our abilities, we unlock the potential for profound change. His journey from a state of burnout and stress to one of fulfillment and alignment with his values underscores the transformative potential within all of us. Steve's story illustrates that by taking ownership of our actions and beliefs, we can shift our life's trajectory toward a more authentic and purposeful existence. Steve's willingness to confront his vulnerabilities and align his actions with his core values led to a remarkable turnaround in his life. This narrative underscores the essence of self-integrity- the alignment of thoughts, actions, and values in harmony.

Living in accordance with our values is not about adhering to a rigid standard of perfection; it's about embracing the process of continuous self-improvement and making choices that reflect our deepest convictions. Every decision to act in harmony with our values, no matter how small, is a step towards reinforcing our self-integrity. This journey of alignment is where we find the true essence of personal development and leadership. It's a path marked by courage, honesty, and unwavering commitment to our authentic selves.

As we navigate our own paths, let Steve's story remind us of the power within each of us to reshape our lives through the choices we make. We earn our self-integrity through these choices, forging a life of authenticity, purpose, and deep self-respect. Remember, the journey towards self-integrity is not about reaching a destination of perfection but about making consistent progress, choosing our values over convenience, and living each day as a true reflection of who we aspire to be. By doing so, you earn your self-respect and inspire those around you to pursue their own paths of self-discovery and transformation. Let the story of Steve and the countless others who have navigated their way through challenges be a reminder that we are all capable of rewriting our narratives, one decision at a time.

Self-integrity is about alignment—thoughts, actions, and ownership of values all in harmony. It's a powerful stance in life that requires courage, honesty, and commitment. The reward is a life of authenticity, purpose, and deep self-respect. This is the path to truly earning yourself.

Go Reflect Yourself Reflection Exercise: Self-Integrity

Now, reflect on your own life. As you reflect, detach your ego from your circumstances. Your financial status, relationships, and possessions don't define you. What defines you is your ability to grow, change, and embrace the full spectrum of your experiences.

Please take a moment to relax your mind. Take a deep breath. This helps calm the 'fight or flight' response, allowing your prefrontal cortex – the rational part of your brain – to engage more effectively in this reflective process.

As you complete this exercise, remember that your current situation doesn't define you. It's merely a starting point for your journey of growth. By embracing radical responsibility, you're not just changing your mindset but rewiring your brain to become the person you aspire to be.

When you look at the key areas in your life, if there are gaps between where you are and where you want to be, it's time to look inward. If your first instinct is to find excuses, pause and think about the role you've played in creating your current reality.

You can request an accompanying self-reflection worksheet by emailing hello@heatherjcrider.com to help you further reflect on radical reflection.

- Have you ever found yourself compromising your desires for others?"

- What happened?

- How did you feel?

- When you are reviewing your own values, what are the first three values that come to mind?

- Why?

Further, explore your values:

- -What are your top two personal values? Why?

- -What are your top two relationship values? Why?

- -What are your top two professional values? Why?

Reflect on Decisions:

Think of a recent decision you made that was aligned with your values.

- How did making this decision based on your values make you feel compared to decisions that weren't as closely aligned?

Assessing Self-Integrity:

- In what areas of your life do you feel you are living in full alignment with your values?

- Where do you see gaps between your values and your actions, and what steps can you take to close those gaps?

Personal Growth and Challenges:

Reflect on a challenge you faced recently.

- How did your response to this challenge align with your core values?

- What did this experience teach you about your capacity for resilience and growth?

<u>Setting Realistic Goals:</u>

Consider a goal you've struggled to achieve.

- To what extent was this goal aligned with your core values?

- How might aligning your goals more closely with your values change your approach to achieving them?

<u>The Role of Vulnerability:</u>

- Reflect on a time when being vulnerable led to personal growth. How did this experience affect your understanding of self-integrity and authenticity?

- Daily Practices for self-Integrity: What daily practices or habits can you adopt to strengthen your self-integrity and ensure your actions align more with your values?

- Learning from failure: Think about a time when you failed to live up to your own expectations. What did this experience teach you about forgiveness, resilience, and the journey toward self-integrity?

- What is one thing you can do each day to prove to yourself you are living in your own integrity?

- After completing this exercise, take a moment to notice what you feel. What emotions surface? What does your body tell you? Write these down, breathe through them, and observe the occurring shifts.

- For the next few days, practice daily reflection. Ask yourself, "What responsibility did I take today?" Whether it's acknowledging a snap at a loved one or recognizing a missed opportunity, it's all about awareness.

- What reflections came up for you when reading this message? What takeaways did you get? How can you apply your takeaways in your life?

Remember, radical responsibility isn't about burdening yourself with blame; it's about empowering yourself to be the architect of your destiny.

As you move forward, remember it's not about perfection. It's about progress, about choosing, again and again, to live in accordance with your values. This is the journey of self-integrity, a journey well worth embarking on.

Chapter Seven

The Alchemy of Thought

"What you think of yourself is much more important than what people think of you." ~ Seneca

T welve years ago, I set out to write a book. It was to be my official launch into the world as a "thought leader." I created an outline, poured my thoughts into a Word document, and was ready to share my insights with the world. I knew I needed an endorsement from a credible author and successful thought leader. So, off I went to an event, armed with a VIP ticket, having flown across the country and printed my manuscript upon arrival, eager for an opportunity to ask for that crucial endorsement.

Seated in the front row, I attended the event, anxious to meet this thought leader at a VIP luncheon. But when the moment came, I froze. Instead of presenting my manuscript, I merely expressed my enjoyment of the event and held onto my work. Feeling defeated, I finished the conference and returned home. There, I discovered a colleague was releasing a book with a similar title to mine. That's when I closed the chapter on that endeavor, relegating my manuscript to a drawer, where it remained untouched for 12 years.

Why did I shelve a project I was so passionate about? Deep down, I lacked belief in myself and my work. Despite numerous accomplishments by that point in my life, my inner dialogue was dominated by fear, uncertainty, and doubt—the FUD whisperer. Instead of trusting in my ability and my story, I doubted my worthiness and the potential impact of my words.

Thoughts like, "This is a silly idea," "This book isn't any good," and the particularly insidious, "Who am I to do this? Why would anyone listen to me?" plagued me. What we think and what we tell ourselves profoundly matter.

Recalling a family interaction years ago, as I was sitting at the breakfast bar at my grandfather's house, my kids, grandfather, and I attempted to play a friendly card game appropriately suited for kids, meaning it was pretty easy. My daughter, a masterful card and game player, led this interaction. Upon explaining the rules and moving forward in the game, my grandfather, who was in his early 80s then, was apprehensive but willing to participate. My son, eager to dive in and master the game instantly at three years old, soon faced a moment of self-doubt. Within minutes of attempting to play the card game, my grandfather declared, 'Well, I'm just too dumb to figure this out.' Then my son looked at me with his giant hazel eyes and, throwing down his cards and in a slightly southern defeated accent, said, 'I just can't do it, Momma, I just can't do it.'

At that moment, my grandfather and my son were limited not by their abilities but by their ingrained self-perceptions.

Although my grandfather had been a very accomplished man with many talents, his upbringing in a dirt-floor home with eight other children in Arkansas and an eighth-grade education led him to fundamentally believe he was dumb his entire life. My son, only three then, hadn't yet accumulated my grandfather's history but had already developed a pattern of defeat. When slightly challenged, he would instantly feel defeated and assume he could not succeed, a tendency he still exhibits. This story of self-doubt, spanning generations, underscores how early and deeply these patterns can form and how they can shape our perception of our capabilities.

In everything we do, whether we are attempting to communicate with a partner, seek engagement from a team, or gain cooperation from a client or customer, the underlying belief in who we are as individuals and the belief in what we do affects how we approach the situations in our lives. Everything boils down to belief: belief in yourself, belief in what you're doing or not. **Belief in what you believe!**

Reflecting on my own journey and the tale of my grandfather and son, we approach a crucial concept: the thought loop. It's a cycle where our feelings, deeply intertwined with our beliefs, shape our thoughts, which in turn drive our actions and mold our outcomes. I've witnessed firsthand in my life how this loop plays out. There have been times when my feelings about myself led to results that brought stress and disappointment. Yet, on the flip side, believing in myself has also led to incredible success. It all comes down to what I believed at the core.

The Thought Loop.

As discussed in Chapter 4, this cycle is a dance of our inner narratives shaping our external world, highlighting the power of our thoughts and beliefs in crafting our reality. When we delve into the thought loop, we're not just exploring an abstract concept; we're looking at a practical tool for transformation. Understanding this loop is about recognizing how our feelings influence our thoughts and actions, steering the outcomes we experience in life.

How we feel affects our thoughts and beliefs, which affect what we say and do, how we respond or react, and our outcomes, consequences, and results. Simply put. Your thoughts affect your life. They affect your current reality and future dreams.

This is critical to understand because how you feel and think about yourself is how you approach everything, whether you realize it or not. Your beliefs about yourself also get projected upon other people as you interact.

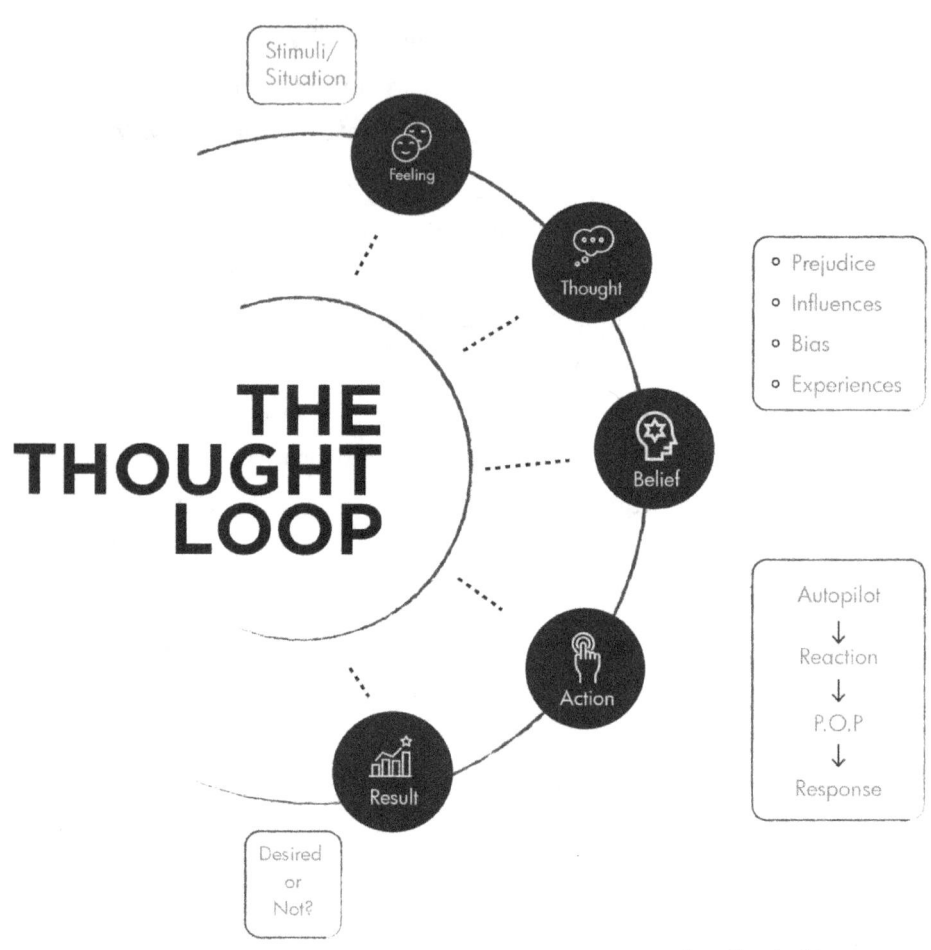

THE
THOUGHT
LOOP

Stimuli/
Situation

Feeling

Thought

Belief

- Prejudice
- Influences
- Bias
- Experiences

Autopilot
↓
Reaction
↓
P.O.P
↓
Response

Action

Result

Desired
or
Not?

www.heatherjcrider.com

"Whether you think you can or you think you can't--you're right." ~ Henry Ford

Words Shape Our Reality

I had a great Uncle who was a huge and confident man. Growing up, he was one of those people who loved to torment me, a common theme when I was a child that I still don't understand. He smoked like a chimney, and he believed he would never be affected by his smoking. He smoked up until he passed away. My grandmother, on the other hand, was a different story. She, too, like her brother, smoked a significant amount her whole life. She believed that her smoking would cause her health issues. She always said it would catch up to her someday, and it did. She developed severe COPD, a chronic lung disease that damages airways. During one particular period when she was in the hospital, I had many conversations with her about her belief in herself getting better and what she could do to help her body heal. No matter the conversation, she ended up defeated and adamantly believed she could not recover. My grandmother, who was my best friend, suffered and quickly passed away from her disease.

Health And Your Thoughts

Many noted psychiatrists and research have shown that positive thinking and a hopeful outlook can improve physical health, enhance recovery, and even extend one's lifespan. This doesn't mean ignoring reality but rather choosing to focus on hope and possibilities.

Psychiatrist Aaron Beck made a groundbreaking discovery while working with his patients: their underlying beliefs were triggering their anxiety and depression. Before a wave of negative emotion hit, thoughts like "Does this doctor think I'm incompetent?" or "This therapy will never work" would flash through their minds. These unconscious beliefs were not only affecting their therapy sessions but their everyday lives as well. Beck realized that by teaching patients to become aware of these fleeting thoughts, he could then help them challenge and change these deep-seated beliefs. This approach laid the foundation for cognitive therapy, which has become one of the most effective forms of treatment. Beck's work illuminated a crucial aspect of the human mind: we continuously process and interpret our experiences, which guides our reactions and decisions. However, when this interpretive process is skewed, it can lead to disproportionate feelings of anxiety, depression, anger, or even a sense of superiority, showing the power of our beliefs to shape our emotional world.

What about placebos?

Sugar pills or placebos have been studied at great length. They are designed to have no medical effect whatsoever to bring any cure. Yet, in almost every control group study using placebo pills, there are some improvements reported, and often as much or more than a group receiving actual medication. Countless studies have reported similar findings when receiving placebos: Students ward off colds, reduction in seasickness among navy members, and even placebo surgery. Another notable research in the field of pain management found that placebo knee surgery, where patients underwent a sham procedure without any actual surgical intervention, resulted in pain relief and improved function comparable to those who had the actual surgery, highlighting the mind's influence over physical health and the powerful influence of belief and expectation on physical health outcomes.

Dr. Maxwell Maltz, the author of "Psycho-Cybernetics," emphasizes the power of self-image and the mind's role in shaping our realities. He suggests that the nervous system cannot differentiate between real and imagined experiences. According to Maltz, this means that imagining success or failure can profoundly impact our actual experiences, as the nervous system responds to both similarly. This principle underlies the "mental rehearsal" concept, where visualizing positive outcomes can enhance performance and improve self-esteem. Maltz advocates for using positive visualizations and affirmations to reprogram the mind for success, arguing that our self-image and beliefs directly influence our actions and outcomes.

To expand on this principle, one of the phrases I repeat frequently with my clients is that your brain cannot distinguish between past, present, or future experiences. My setup is if you want to achieve something, feel as if it has already happened. This concept suggests that when we visualize or imagine an event, the brain activates similarly to when we actually experience that event. This phenomenon is grounded in the brain's network activation patterns, where imagining an action stimulates many of the same neural pathways as performing the action.

Neuroscience supports this through studies on visualization and mental rehearsal, showing that athletes or performers who vividly imagine their performance can enhance their actual performance, akin to physical practice. This is because the sensory and motor cortexes involved in physical action activate during vivid mental rehearsal. The brain's plasticity allows these mental practices to strengthen neural pathways, improving motor skills and performance without physical execution.

Moreover, the emotional response to imagined scenarios can be as strong as responses to actual events, influencing our mood, stress levels, and even physiological states.

Therefore, suggesting that whether you think you can or cannot, you are right.

Every thought you think changes your life and rewires your brain. You get to choose how you want to rewire your brain.

Neuroplasticity

In Chapter 2, I brought up the concept of neuroplasticity, where you can change the pathways in your brain. When reflecting on thoughts and their power in our outcomes, it is essential to understand neuroplasticity further. Specifically, Dr. Shad Helmstetter's work on self-talk and neuroplasticity explains the critical insight into how the language we use with ourselves, our internal dialogue, directly influences our brain's wiring and, consequently, our behaviors, emotions, and outcomes.

Helmstetter suggests that the brain is malleable and can be reprogrammed through consistent, positive self-talk. By actively choosing our thoughts and the words we say to ourselves, we engage in a form of mental training that can alter our neural pathways. This process, rooted in the principles of neuroplasticity, implies that repeated positive or negative self-talk can strengthen specific neural networks, leading to lasting changes in our thought patterns, beliefs, and behaviors.

For example, if we continuously tell ourselves that we are capable and resilient, these affirmations can help build neural pathways that enhance our self-esteem and coping skills. Conversely, negative self-talk can reinforce pathways that contribute to anxiety and self-doubt.

Helmstetter's work underscores the importance of being mindful of our internal dialogue, as it can shape our brain's structure and function, influencing our overall well-being and capacity to achieve our goals. Or, in my grandfather's case, his lifelong habit of calling himself stupid and believing he is stupid. Or, in my grandmother's case, believing her smoking would catch up to her.

Another way I typically explain it is this. Imagine your brain is a forest filled with paths. These paths are your habits and thoughts. Walking the same path—like a belief or habit—makes it well-worn and easy to follow. But when you decide to change a belief or form a new habit, it's like forging a new path through the underbrush. At first, it's challenging, unfamiliar, painful, and full of thorns and weeds, but the more you travel this new path, the clearer and easier it becomes. This is neuroplasticity in action—your brain's ability to form new connections and pathways. Start by catching negative thoughts as they arise and consciously choose to redirect them towards something positive. It's like choosing a new path in the forest of your mind—one that leads to a healthier, happier you.

Existential vs Experiential

What about the now, and how do our emotions play into this pathway-building?

Every now and again, I catch myself saying, "I think I'm having an existential crisis"! What a dramatic statement, I realize.

I have learned to recognize that when I say, "I think I'm having an existential crisis," there is something deeper that I need to reflect on.

I realized during these moments that I felt overwhelmed and lacked control. I may be taking on too much responsibility, or other factors contribute to my feeling this way. But what sets up this feeling for me is the overuse of existential language that creates a pattern and a feeling that I am something. Because our brain has a natural negativity bias, anything that supports this negativity craving gets bolstered.

If I spend a week saying how stupid "I am," my thoughts, feelings, habits, and behaviors will attempt to support the I am statement. As subtle as it might sound, shifting your language and deep feelings from "I am stupid" to "I am feeling disappointed in myself" makes all the difference to how you view yourself and how your brain supports you differently. However, it is challenging to sort out your feelings when you are in the middle of a brain hijack.

I know when my children are arguing, and I'm in the middle of balancing all the mountain of tasks to be dealt with, schedules to adhere to, clients to respond to, and staff to check in with, my head is swimming with emotions, and I lose it sometimes. To have emotions is a profoundly human element we all experience.

Lisa Feldman Barrett, a psychologist who focuses on how emotions form, has decoded some of the scientific complexity of understanding emotions. She explains that our brains need to label emotions in the form of telling itself a story to interrupt what is happening to the body about what's happening around us. The story creates an understanding of an emotion that you have learned from an experience to be able to predict an outcome and forecast what you see and hear in the future. Essentially, the brain keeps track of events based on all the data it collects internally as it relates to the external environment.

Emotions come from bodily sensations as well as how our brain interprets those body sensations. Barrett proposes that emotions are not pre-wired reactions but rather constructed by the brain based on past experiences, the current situation, and our goals. In short, she believes we don't "decode" emotions from universal expressions but rather "construct" them based on diverse inputs. This means we are NOT our emotions; instead, we are experiencing emotions based on our brain's response to the world around us.

Because emotions help your brain respond, labeling will move you from the existential versus experiential to distinguish you as the being and you as the being who is experiencing a specific emotion. Another way of putting it is that we are not our thoughts; we are the thinkers of our thoughts.

<u>For example:</u>

I am so angry that my mother hung up the phone on me. She is so childish, and it makes me angry.

I am sad that my partner canceled our plans.

I am furious that my boss didn't give me a raise. How awful of her.

I am so stupid for yelling at my assistant the other day. She did something really dumb, and I was angry and yelled at her, but I am stupid for doing it.

Attaching our existential selves to our feelings makes the emotion more intense, personal, and challenging. Changing our emotions is not about directly forcing ourselves to feel differently. Instead, to be in more control and choose more wisely.

Action Versus Being

Expand your emotional vocabulary to describe your feelings more precisely. By having more specific words to identify your emotions, you gain a deeper understanding of your experience. Instead of simply saying "I feel bad," you might identify it as "frustrated," "disappointed," or "overwhelmed." Or "I am so stupid," say, "I felt disappointed in how I handled this situation."

Reframe The Experience

Instead of staying in "Disappointment or frustration," you might reframe it as a signal that you need to adjust your approach or seek a different state in managing a particular situation. This shift in perspective can influence how you interpret the situation and, ultimately, your emotional response.

For example: You may notice that when your mother calls, you get tense, lack concentration, and feel frustrated, angry, or upset. Instead of staying in this state, you can notice and reframe. You can seek a different way of approaching when she calls. Or only take the call during certain times.

It's important to remember that changing emotions is a gradual process that requires practice and self-compassion. Dr. Barrett emphasizes that emotions are not inherently good or bad, and focusing on accepting and understanding them is the first step toward effective modification.

Keep in mind the self-deprecating words and emotions. Specifically, when you stay in patterns of harm for yourself, saying "I am stupid," or "I will never achieve my goals,"...The more you repeat these phrases and attach your identity to them, the more you believe them, and your brain will seek to fulfill these beliefs. Reflecting on your default statements about yourself and others is very powerful.

Back when my son said he couldn't do it. I would say to him, "I believe you". Not because I believe you cannot, but because you say you cannot, and when you say you cannot, you already believe that to be true.

How you feel when you show up will affect how you approach what you are doing and trying to accomplish.

Why Am I...

Helmstetter's research provides a scientific foundation for why and how changing our words and thoughts can transform our lives. By understanding and applying the principles of neuroplasticity, we can consciously influence our mental landscape, turning challenges into opportunities for growth and fostering a positive mindset that supports our journey toward excellence and extraordinariness. How you view your identity and self-concept comes from the deep belief about your self-worth and self-confidence. One method of applying neuroplasticity principles is to explore how you talk to yourself.

The concept of affirmations is a traditional theory to speak in an affirmative way to change how you view yourself. Neuroimaging studies show that self-affirmation can activate reward pathways in the brain and parts associated with self-processing. This suggests there's a neurological basis for the potential effects.

An additional theory exists that traditional affirmations can cause discord. For example, a conventional affirmation such as "I am wealthy" often fails because it can clash with subconscious beliefs. When your mind senses a contradiction, it triggers a "yeah, right" response that undermines the affirmation. However, positive statements can have positive results on our thoughts; they can sometimes backfire as well.

Thought leader Noah St. John created what he calls AF-FORMATIONS®, which consists of The Power of Questions. He suggests asking empowering "why" questions, e.g., "Why am I so wealthy?" instead of "I am" statements. He argues that when you ask questions, you bypass the brain's automatic skepticism and force your mind to search for answers that support the desired belief. And I would agree with his assessment.

Your brain's natural propensity is to seek answers to questions and even is compelled to seek the answer when presented with questions.

It's a physiological phenomenon. When someone asks you a question, even if it is a rhetorical question, you have a desire and are almost compelled to want to answer it, consciously or subconsciously!

Asking 'why' questions is one of the keys to unlocking your superpowers.

Neuroscience Nerd Out Moment:

You prime the Reticular Activating System (RAS) by focusing on a question. RAS is a network of neurons located in the brainstem. It acts as a filter for the massive amount of information our senses collect from the external environment, determining what information is important enough to be processed by the brain. The RAS helps prioritize attention and focus, allowing us to concentrate on specific stimuli while ignoring others that are deemed less important, aiding in goal setting and motivation.

Ways to Explore "Why Questions"

The premise is that by repeatedly asking empowering questions, you reprogram your subconscious thought patterns, paving the way for changes in your beliefs and behavior.

Afformations use "why" questions instead of positive statements like traditional affirmations. This can encourage reflection and exploration rather than simply repeating statements that may not resonate with your current beliefs.

By asking, "Why am I confident?" you engage your mind to actively search for evidence and reasons to support a positive self-image, aligning with the experiential perspective where self-perception is constructed through ongoing internal processes.

Shift from "being" to "becoming": Traditional affirmations often use phrases like "I am confident," which emphasizes a static state. Afformations might ask, "Why am I becoming more confident?" This subtle shift acknowledges that self-perception is not fixed but rather an ongoing journey, reflecting the dynamic nature of the experiential perspective.

Address limiting beliefs: The "why" in Afformations can lead you to identify underlying negative beliefs hindering your self-image. By acknowledging and questioning these limitations, you can actively challenge them and create space for more positive self-perceptions, aligning with the experiential perspective's emphasis on reinterpreting your experience.

Chapter Summary:

The Power of Belief and Self-Talk: One of the core messages is the profound impact our beliefs and the conversations we have with ourselves have on our lives. Whether it's overcoming self-doubt, as illustrated by my story of shelving a book project or witnessing generational patterns of self-limiting beliefs, we are reminded how our internal dialogues shape our actions, outcomes, and overall life trajectories.

Understanding and Navigating the Thought Loop: The Thought Loop concept emphasizes the cyclical nature of how our feelings influence our thoughts, beliefs, actions, and, ultimately, our results. This takeaway underscores the importance of being mindful of our internal narratives and learning to positively influence this cycle to foster better outcomes and personal growth.

The Impact of Words and Neuroplasticity: The words we use and the thoughts we entertain not only reflect our current reality but also have the power to shape our brains and future. Neuroplasticity enables the brain to form new connections, allowing affirmations and afformations to influence behavior and beliefs. By consistently applying these techniques, you can rewire your brain to support positive self-perception and the pursuit of excellence.

Starting Your Day on the Right Note: The first thoughts upon waking can have a positive or negative mindset that can influence the entire day's trajectory. Be conscious of your initial thoughts and actively choose positivity, setting a foundation for a day aligned with your goals and aspirations.

Go Reflect Yourself Reflection Exercise: Alchemy of Thought

Superpower Your Thoughts

Consider the paths you've worn in the forest of your mind. Are they leading you to where you want to be? If not, remember it's never too late to start forging a new path.

There is a lot to unpack in the Alchemy of Thought chapter! Mindfully consider the following questions and answer what you feel is most important right now!

1. What was your first thought this morning when you woke up?

2. Why did you think that thought?

3. Did that thought serve you or propel you forward in your day?

4. Did that thought slow you down, drain you, or define your day in a way that did not serve you?

5. When you start your day in a frame of mind that does not support who you are or what you want to accomplish, how does it affect your actions and behavior throughout the day?

6. Each morning for the next three days, write down the first thought you think. If it's positive and healthy, great. If it is not, how can you immediately change and shift your thought?

7. Reflect on how your subconscious feelings influence your actions and behaviors. When you feel dread, how does it manifest in your daily activities?

8. How have my beliefs about myself influenced my actions and decisions in the past?

9. Ask, Can I identify a specific instance where negative self-talk held me back from pursuing a goal or opportunity?

10. What is one belief I hold about myself that I would like to change, and why?

11. How can I apply the concept of neuroplasticity to re-shape this belief?

12. Reflecting on the Thought Loop, what is a recurring thought pattern I notice, and how does it affect my emotions and behaviors?

13. What positive affirmations can I start incorporating into my daily routine to reinforce empowering beliefs?

14. How does understanding the role of the Reticular Activating System (RAS) change my perspective on focusing attention and setting goals?

15. Can I think of an example when a placebo effect (or the power of belief) manifested in my own life or someone I know?

16. What new path do I want to forge in the "forest" of my mind, and what are the first steps to making this path more traveled?

17. How can expanding my emotional vocabulary and re-framing my experiences help me manage my emotions more effectively?

These questions encourage reflection on how your thoughts and beliefs shape your reality and aim to guide you toward a more empowering and positive mindset.

Make your own list of AFFORMATIONS:

Here are a few to start with:

1. Why am I capable of achieving my dreams?

2. Why do I feel so confident in my abilities?

3. Why am I finding it easy to overcome obstacles?

4. Why am I so grateful for everything I have?

5. Why do I attract positivity and success effortlessly?

6. Why am I so effective at communicating my needs and desires?

7. Why do I feel so loved and supported by those around me?

8. Why am I consistently making choices that align with my highest good?

9. Why am I so motivated and productive every day?

10. Why do I find joy and satisfaction in my daily activities?

11. Why am I so skilled at navigating difficult conversations with ease and confidence?

12. Why do I naturally inspire and motivate my team, even in challenging times?

13. Why am I so adept at finding win-win solutions in my business dealings?

14. Why do I attract cooperative and supportive colleagues and business partners?

15. Why am I so effective at managing my emotions, even in high-stress situations?

16. Why do I communicate my business ideas so clearly and persuasively?

17. Why am I so successful at fostering a positive and

productive work environment?

18. Why do I easily understand and empathize with others' perspectives, enhancing my leadership?

19. Why am I consistently able to exceed my business goals with the support of my team?

20. Why do I thrive in negotiations, always achieving the best outcome for my business and team?

Chapter Eight

Empowerment Through Action

"Nothing will work unless you do," ~ Maya Angelou

Maya Angelou once wisely remarked, "Nothing will work unless you do," a sentiment that resonates deeply, especially when we say, "I don't want to." Take my son, for instance, who expressed this sentiment one evening at the prospect of homework, a task universally acknowledged as less than thrilling. This reluctance isn't exclusive to children; we often balk at specific adult responsibilities. Reflecting on my early days as a corporate accountant tasked with late-night report completions, I recall my exhaustion and intimidation by the workload. Back then, my inefficiency wasn't just about resisting the tasks at hand; I wore my late nights like a badge of honor, mistakenly equating long hours with hard work. However, this approach, fueled by apprehension and strain, only diminished my effectiveness, unnecessarily prolonging my hours.

What You Resist Persists

As highlighted in the Reflection ABCs, awareness is fundamental to self-empowerment and belief. While previous chapters have delved into the intricacies of emotions, patterns, beliefs, and thoughts, the notion of resistance is one area we still need to explore in depth. Resistance, in essence, is informative—a gift, even. It presents itself as a beacon in our evolutionary journey, much like uncovering layers in an archaeological dig. With each layer comes both excitement and, potentially, a new set of challenges. Despite the increasing difficulty, this process of discovery and the desire to delve deeper mirrors our journey of self-exploration. It's a testament to the fact that no part of this exploration is inherently negative; rather, it's all valuable information.

Despite having confidently presented on stage to hundreds since my college days, the thought of hosting a live session on social media filled me with an inexplicable dread. Online presentations and social media live were different beasts altogether. On stage, I felt in control, the immediate feedback from the audience fueling my energy. But facing a camera for a live online event, where the audience's reactions were hidden behind screens, felt daunting. I feared the immediacy of judgment, the potential for technical glitches, and the vulnerability of being "seen" in such an unfiltered way. Why did this terrify me when I had faced larger audiences in person?

I repeatedly put off scheduling my first live session, citing reasons ranging from not having the perfect topic to waiting for better lighting equipment—excuses that thinly veiled my fear of failure and looking foolish. But as my avoidance grew, so did the realization that I was hindering my growth. My resistance was a barrier not just to potential opportunities but to personal development.

Finally, I took the plunge. I scheduled my first live session on social media, announcing it publicly to ensure there was no backing out. The anticipation was nerve-wracking, but once I went live, a transformation occurred. Yes, there were hiccups—a moment when I lost my train of thought and a technical glitch briefly interrupted the stream—but they were far from catastrophic. The feedback was overwhelmingly positive, with viewers appreciating the authenticity and value of the content.

This experience was enlightening. My resistance had magnified my fears, making the prospect of going live seem insurmountable. Yet, facing it head-on not only dispelled those fears but also opened a new avenue for connecting with my audience. The difference wasn't in the medium but in my approach to it. Embracing the vulnerability of live presentations allowed me to expand my reach and impact in ways I had not anticipated. It taught me that what we resist not only persists but also holds us back from exploring new horizons.

The essence of what I term the 'Abundance Activator' revolves around perceiving everything as a gift of information. Embracing this perspective allows us to adapt, evolve, and make informed decisions. When we begin to view our challenges and resistances as opportunities for growth, we feel a certain lightness—a sense of aliveness that renders us unstoppable. We aim for this vibrancy, as it embodies the peak of empowerment and action. I find this concept of abundance particularly exhilarating, for it sheds light on the liberating aspect of enlightenment. One of my core client pieces of training explores the abundance activator in-depth as a part of my core transformational program, and if you want to experience it for yourself, contact my team at hello@heatherjcrider.com.

"Motivation Doesn't Last. Neither Does Bathing. That's Why We Recommend it Daily." Zig Ziglar

Borrow It, Fake It, Believe It

Tessa, one of my mentors, embodies positivity and wisdom. Her influence extends far and wide, touching everyone she meets with a spark of uplifting spirit. During a particularly challenging period with one of my businesses, compounded by personal turmoil, I was in a state of self-doubt and frustration. Conversations with Tessa often circled back to my lack of self-belief. Despite understanding the realm of possibilities that dreams and goals offer, my experiences left me feeling deflated.

Tessa offered me a unique perspective: the concept of borrowing belief. She, like my grandmother, had an unwavering belief in my potential. She suggested that when my belief falters, I could lean on the belief others have in me as a temporary scaffold while I worked on reconstructing my own. This idea resonated deeply with me, offering a beacon of hope amidst my self-doubt.

My Uncle Winston was another pillar of support, embodying patience and an unshakeable belief in my capabilities. His approach was never about instilling false hope but genuinely encouraging me to adopt his belief in me during my moments of uncertainty. His calm assurance was a reminder to focus on progress and possibilities rather than being mired in feelings of regret or inadequacy.

Embracing Tessa and Uncle Winston's belief in me, I began to see a shift in my mindset. In times of doubt and being overwhelmed, I've borrowed their belief, my grandmother's belief, and anyone else's I could. Borrowing their belief was a powerful stepping stone, enabling me to rebuild my belief in myself gradually. This journey taught me the transformative power of borrowed belief, guiding me to look "onward and upward" and move beyond the confines of sorrow and self-doubt. **However, what about when I just don't feel up to it?**

I Don't Feel Like It

Some days, the motivation just isn't there. As a single working mom of two for over a decade, there are plenty of moments when the phrase "I just don't feel like it" echoes through my mind.

Being human requires a tremendous amount of emotional energy. On top of personal challenges, there's the task of growing a business and the relentless pace of raising two children. And then there's the dog, although calling her the most emotionally taxing might be overstating it a bit. Sure, she adds another layer of responsibility, but perhaps she's more man-ageable than managing a business or parenting.

This constant juggling act of personal and professional obligations can be overwhelming. It's a sentiment many can relate to, the feeling of being stretched too thin, of having too much on your plate. Yet, despite the exhaustion and the occasional lack of motivation, there's a more profound under-standing that each of these roles and responsibilities enriches life in unique ways. It's about finding the balance, the drive, and sometimes, the simple act of showing up, even when you don't feel like it, that makes all the difference. Or sometimes, faking it until you make it.

FAKE IT

Initially, I harbored skepticism toward the notion of "faking it until you make it." To me, it smacked of hypocrisy, a way of presenting oneself that felt fundamentally at odds with my quest for authenticity and genuine self-expression. However, my perspective shifted dramatically through encounters and reflections, particularly through my observations and conver-sations with Murl.

Sometimes, it's about faking it until you make it.

I'll never forget my first encounter with Murl at the hair salon where he was a new addition. His spirit was immediately captivating. At the salon, his duties ranged from sweeping floors to greeting guests with an unmistakable warmth. But it wasn't just his tasks—handing out arm massages, making small talk—that struck me; it was his unabashed joy and authentic-ity. To some, Murl's appearance and demeanor, possibly influenced by his sexual orientation, might have been unsettling or even controversial. Yet, I believe we all yearn to embody a similar confidence and authenticity, though the path there often eludes us.

Observing him over the years, I was always taken by his immediate effort to compliment everyone he met, embodying a principle straight from John Maxwell's playbook on winning people over within seconds. Murl's ability to put himself out there, regardless of whether this was a learned behavior or an innate talent, was something I deeply admired. Watching his journey from a salon helper to a fully-fledged stylist, I witnessed his professional growth and personal evolution into the vibrant individual he is today.

A recent conversation with Murl shed new light on his journey. All those years of admiring his confidence, I was oblivious to the internal battle he faced. He confessed that despite appearing authentic, he often felt like an imposter, hiding behind a facade of 'fakeness.' This revelation was a stark reminder that our insecurities are universal, each of us grappling with our own fears, uncertainties, and doubts.

During our talk, Murl shared how he intentionally compliments people, knowing too well the sting of insecurity. He believes that if he can make someone feel good, even for a moment, he's not only exposing his own vulnerabilities but also encouraging others to embrace theirs. This practice, he discovered, was not just about making others feel seen; it was a pathway to his empowerment and strength. By choosing to be vulnerable, Murl found a profound sense of self-assurance and authenticity. Each time I encounter Murl, even if I speak to him directly, I am uplifted by his spirit and willingness to take a leap to help others feel more confident, all starting with a simple compliment.

Murl's story is a testament to the power of "faking it till you make it." This approach helped him navigate his insecurities, enabling him to project confidence and authenticity until they became his reality. Such stories inspire me because they underscore a universal truth: we all face adversity and have our own insecurities to conquer.

Reflecting on this, I've now come to see "faking it till you make it" not as hypocrisy but instead as a tool for personal growth and empowerment. It's about adopting a posture of confidence and belief in oneself, even when we're not quite there yet, to catalyze the transformation we seek. This mindset has become a critical component of my approach to fostering a belief in my abilities and the empowerment that follows. Through embracing this philosophy, I've learned that sometimes, supporting your own belief and empowerment means stepping into the role you aspire to fill, even before you feel fully ready.

Empowerment Through Action

A Guide to Transforming Aspirations into Tangible Outcomes: How You Do Anything Is How You Do Everything.

This adage reminds us that our approach to small tasks reflects our approach to life's more significant challenges. It's not just about what we do but how we do it—with dedication, attention to detail, and integrity. Consider the late nights spent working on a daunting project, viewing it not as a burden but as an opportunity to showcase resilience and efficiency. Or, think about a difficult interaction with a colleague or guiding a child through a challenging moment—holding your power and responding with patience and wisdom. Each action, no matter how small, from how we handle conflict to how we complete daily tasks, is a testament to our character and approach to life. It's about shifting our mindset from resisting work to embracing it as a chance for growth, leading to not only improved productivity but also personal satisfaction and empowerment.

Understanding Resistance as a Pathway to Growth

Awareness of our emotions and patterns is the first step toward self-empowerment. Recognizing resistance—not as an obstacle but as information—provides valuable insights into our fears and apprehensions. This perspective is like an archeological dig through the layers of our psyche, where each layer uncovered presents both a challenge and an opportunity for deeper understanding and growth. By acknowledging and working through resistance, we discover our resilience and ability to adapt, setting the stage for transformation and empowerment.

Actionable Insights: Turning Challenges into Opportunities

Leadership in action means seeing beyond problems to envision potential outcomes and solutions. Successful leaders and individuals recognize that problems are inevitable but surmountable with the right mindset and actions. Embracing challenges as opportunities for learning and growth changes our relationship with adversity, allowing us to move past it more swiftly and effectively.

For example, committing to running a marathon might seem daunting, but breaking it down into manageable training goals transforms an overwhelming challenge into a series of achievable steps. This approach not only builds momentum but also reinforces our belief in our capabilities.

Commitment and Integrity: The Cornerstones of Empowerment

Our commitments, both to ourselves and others, reflect our integrity. Just as we must be honest with ourselves about our capabilities and limits, we must also be truthful in our commitments. If we overcommit and fail to deliver, it erodes trust and undermines our self-confidence. Conversely, by setting realistic goals and consistently meeting them, we build a strong foundation of trust and character. This is the essence of empowerment: knowing that we are as good as our word and our actions align with our values.

Weekly Challenge:

1. Reflect on Your Commitments: Examine your commitments for the week. Are they aligned with your capabilities and values?

2. Embrace Problems as Opportunities: When faced with a challenge, ask yourself what you can learn. How can you turn this problem into an opportunity for growth?

3. Act with Integrity: Ensure that your actions reflect your commitments. If you've promised to take on a task, do it to the best of your ability. Remember, building trust with others starts with being trustworthy to yourself.

Developing the Toolbox for Action

Allison, a long-time client of mine, struggled significantly when we first began our work together. Her emotional reactions and frequent brain hijacks were not only affecting her business but also her health, relationships, and overall quality of life. Despite knowing the tools, she often asked, "What tool can I use?" Yet, she resisted using them. Why? Because staying in the same pattern, resisting change, and complaining was easier for her.

She knew what needed to be done but lacked the belief to take action. Allison had the toolbox and the skills; however, she preferred to remain stuck in her comfortable patterns rather than utilize the tools she had learned. This scenario is a common roadblock many face.

A new client, a business leader, encountered similar challenges. As he was thrust into a new role filled with new tasks, a fresh team, and increased responsibilities, he found himself in the very situation he had always aspired to. Yet, with these new challenges came the need for a new skill set. Instead of staying stuck, together, we developed a comprehensive plan to address his obstacles—a sound strategy. Nevertheless, he, too, resisted.

The core issue for both clients wasn't laziness or a lack of intelligence. The problem was their mind acting as a servant to old habits and patterns rather than as a master to new, more constructive behaviors. Our minds, while exceptional servants, can become terrible masters if left unchecked, clinging to comfort even if it means adhering to detrimental habits. Mastery over one's mind requires practice and deliberate action.

Building Your Toolbox

To overcome these challenges, it's crucial to develop a personal toolbox—a collection of strategies, habits, and skills tailored to managing emotional responses and fostering positive change. This toolbox isn't just about knowing what tools are available; it's about believing in yourself to use them effectively and choosing to step out of your comfort zone to implement change.

I mentioned the brain hijack in earlier chapters, most descriptively in Chapter 4. Understanding how a brain hijack works is great, especially when you're not currently experiencing one. But what do you do when you're in the throes of a hijack or when deep distrust, disbelief, or a persistent emotion blocks your path forward? The solution isn't merely to dodge these hijacks but to be adept in deploying the right tools at the right time. With consistent practice, your aim is to diminish the intensity of these responses, recognize the signs of an emotional takeover, and recover more swiftly, allowing you to respond with greater wisdom. By regaining control, you effectively tap into your superpowers—those innate abilities that empower you to face challenges head-on with resilience and clarity.

One of the initial steps I take with clients involves crafting a personalized toolkit. This collection of strategies and practices is not static; it evolves as you do, becoming more potent with regular use. These tools are not just about managing moments of high emotion but are designed to refine your ability to perceive the onset of such states, enabling preemptive action. Think of it as honing your superpowers: the more you engage with these tools, the more adept you become at navigating emotional scenarios, transforming potential weaknesses into strengths.

By leaning into calm, making decisions with a clear mind, and acting courageously, you're not just reacting; you're proactively engaging with your inner strengths. This approach requires not just understanding but embodying the principles of emotional intelligence and resilience. Each time you successfully navigate a challenging situation by employing your toolkit, you're not merely overcoming a hurdle but reinforcing your superpowers, building them up to be stronger and more reliable.

This journey of building superpowers is just like training any muscle; it requires dedication, repetition, and a willingness to push through discomfort. The tools in your personal toolkit—whether they involve mindfulness practices, cognitive reframing, or physiological techniques to calm the nervous system—are your exercises. Regularly applying these tools, especially in moments of calm, prepares you for the moments of storm. As you develop these superpowers, you'll find that you recover more quickly from emotional hijacks and begin to navigate life with a deeper sense of confidence, resilience, and emotional agility.

In the next few pages, you can choose from several exercises and action plans to help you achieve your belief superpowers. Are you ready? Let's go!

Mindfulness and Awareness:

Where your attention goes, your energy flows, whether you want it to or not.

The brain's tendency to default to autopilot mode can sidetrack us from our intended path, leading to reactions and decisions that may not serve our best interests. For example, when faced with stress, it's easy to slip into familiar habits, like mindlessly scrolling through social media or snacking, instead of addressing the root cause of our feelings. Fueled by past experiences and fears, this autopilot reaction detracts from our ability to live in the moment and make choices aligned with our goals.

Consider mindfulness practice to shift from this automatic mode to a state of mindful awareness. Mindfulness allows us to pause, observe our current state, and choose responses that align with our intentions. Imagine you're working on a project and starting to feel overwhelmed. Instead of automatically reaching for your phone for a distraction, you take a deep breath, recognize the signs of stress, and decide to take a short walk or practice a few minutes of deep breathing. This simple act of mindfulness redirects your attention from ruminating on stress to focusing on the present, enabling you to return to your task with a clearer mind and a more focused intention.

Mindful awareness strengthens our ability to control where our attention goes, ensuring our energy flows towards actions and thoughts that are in harmony with our personal objectives and values. By cultivating this awareness, we can break the cycle of autopilot reactions and embrace choices that propel us toward our desired outcomes, enhancing our well-being and productivity.

Understanding the brain's natural default to an autopilot reaction to situations around us will help to break the cycle when the autopilot is not taking you to the location you want to go. The illustration below summarizes the process, where your attention can get caught ruminating or projecting fear based on memories. Your attention can get distracted, causing you to be less aware of the current situation and react in a way that does not align with your goals. Mindful awareness is critical to help strengthen the autopilot response and allow you to choose a desired outcome.

Combatting Everyday Mind for More Resilience

The practice of mindfulness is just that, its practice. My own practice alters from moment to moment, day to day. Some days, I am incredibly mindful, and some days, I am more distracted than a squirrel in a yard full of oak trees. This is the summation of the human condition. Full of opportunities to practice. The goal of achieving mindfulness is not to become a bald man in a robe sitting cross-legged on a mountaintop. However, for me, that is a peaceful scene.

Mindfulness is not the ability to have a euphoric life at every moment; it is to recognize, accept, and savor each moment because all we have is this moment in time.

My partner and amazing keynote speaker, Mark Schulman, created the phrase "Life is a series of nows." All we have is now. Accept the now—party with the now.

Embracing Daily Habits and Non-Negotiables

An essential aspect of managing our monkey mind involves establishing daily habits or "non-negotiables" that support our mental and emotional well-being. These are activities or practices that, regardless of how our day unfolds, we commit to completing. They could range from walking, getting some sunshine, exercising, or even ensuring we stay hydrated. Perhaps going to bed at a specific time, eating a particular meal, or performing a certain task each day is part of your non-negotiables.

The aim is to identify two key non-negotiables that resonate with us personally, serving as anchors in our daily lives. One of the ways to achieve the non-negotiables is to develop a practice I suggest for my clients, which is to develop what I call the daily 10.

What are two things that last 10 minutes you can do each day?

- A 10-minute walk?

- A 10-minute meditation?

- A 10-minute journaling session?

- A 10-minute power workout?

- A 10-minute reading time?

- A 10-minute service time?

Keep a list of ten daily options, and ensure you actively perform two of them each day.

What are your Daily Non-Negotiables?

Expanding on the daily habits section emphasizes the significance of establishing consistent routines supporting mental and emotional well-being. These practices, or "non-negotiables," are the foundation for a balanced and productive day, ensuring that certain essential activities are completed regardless of external pressures or challenges.

Here's an enhanced look at incorporating daily habits for sustained well-being:

<u>Example Daily Habits for Sustained Well-Being</u>

Morning Rituals

- Practice: Begin daily with a morning ritual that energizes and centers you. This could be a short meditation, making your bed, a gratitude journaling session, an energizing workout, or a gentle yoga flow. The key is to engage in activities that set a positive tone for the day ahead.

- Impact: Morning rituals can significantly improve your mood, increase productivity, and provide a sense of calm throughout the day. They help mentally prepare for the day's tasks, fostering a mindset equipped to handle challenges gracefully.

Physical Activity for Vitality

- Practice: Incorporate 15-30 minutes of physical activity into your day, whether it's a brisk walk, a workout session, or cycling. The activity doesn't need to be intense; the goal is to move your body and stimulate your heart rate.

- Impact: Regular physical activity boosts energy levels, improves mood by releasing endorphins, and contributes to overall physical health and brain health. It's also a powerful stress reliever, helping to clear the mind and enhance focus.

Mindful Breaks

- Practice: Schedule short, mindful breaks throughout your day to disconnect and recharge. This could involve stepping outside for fresh air, practicing deep breathing exercises, or enjoying a brief mindfulness meditation. (Picking a daily 10). Set a mindfulness clock on your phone or computer every hour to practice a mindful break.

- Impact: Taking mindful breaks helps prevent burnout, reduces stress, and improves concentration. It allows you to return to your tasks with renewed focus and energy, making you more effective and less prone to fatigue.

Evening Wind-Down for Quality Rest:

- Practice: Establish an evening routine that signals your body that it's time to wind down. This might include dimming the lights, turning off electronic devices an hour before bed, reading a book, or taking a warm bath.

- Impact: A calming evening routine enhances the quality of your sleep, which is crucial for recovery, emotional regulation, and cognitive function. A good sleep routine ensures you wake up refreshed and ready for the new day and allows your brain time to purge and reset for focus and productivity.

Reflective Practice for Personal Growth

- Practice: Dedicate time each evening to reflect on your day. Consider what went well, what challenges you encountered, and what lessons you can carry forward. This can be done through journaling or quiet contemplation.

- Impact: Reflective practice fosters personal growth, emotional resilience, and a deeper understanding of oneself. It encourages a proactive approach to life, where challenges are viewed as opportunities for learning and self-improvement.

Making these practices non-negotiable parts of your daily routine creates a stable foundation for surviving and thriving in your personal and professional life. They serve as pillars that support your overall well-being, enabling you to approach life with a sense of purpose, clarity, and vitality.

MEDITATION:

"Meditation is a way of being in touch with reality. It is a way of waking up to the beauty and wonder of life, no matter what the circumstances." Thich Nhat Hanh

Regardless of what's happening around you, learning to be present and connected to life is a common goal we seek. The core goal of meditation is to help you become present and connected to life around you at that moment, in the moment. But what's happening around us is what often holds us back from meditating at all. Most of us don't actually mediate, regardless of what's happening. When things are going great, and we feel happy, we don't meditate because we forget and don't feel like it's important at the moment. When we're caught in chaos or feeling unhappy, we don't meditate because we forget the value and feel like meditating is worthless at that time. The key to meditation is to meditate, regardless of what's happening. Doing so helps us remain connected and present. Meditation can be simple if we choose it to be.

Sit. Notice. Accept.

It's that simple. Meditation doesn't have to be complicated or dreadful. The goal isn't to force anything to happen, either. The goal is to simply sit and be. Be present. Feel what you feel. If nothing comes up for you, great. If something else comes up for you, great. If you get distracted, great. Embrace it all. Most of my clients have come to me at one point or another, frustrated and feeling defeated because they felt like they were doing meditation wrong. They felt like no matter how hard they tried. They couldn't figure out this meditation thing. The key is to try. The key is to do it. It's not how hard you try nor how perfectly you are doing it; it's just the simple fact of doing it. Just like going to the gym, showing up is half the battle. It is a luxury and the chance to do nothing! Embrace the nothingness!

In an earlier chapter, I described how the monkey mind is a common distraction most of us face. It is a natural part of meditation for your mind to wander and the monkey mind to take over. As odd as it sounds, it's a good thing when it does wander so you can catch it. When you catch the monkey mind and notice that it is present, the act of noticing is helping you re-train your awareness.

Meditation doesn't have to be as challenging as we make it. You can meditate while you're walking. You can meditate while you're eating or even while you're working. Sit in a chair. Sit on the floor. Sit outside. Lay down on the ground. Sit on the ground like a little kid with your legs in the air against a couch; it doesn't matter.

Three ways you can meditate for two minutes or less.

The next time you walk to your mailbox and check your mail, I invite you to walk as slowly as possible. As you walk, feeling your feet beneath you, feeling the ground, what does it feel like feeling your shoes? How do your feet feel in your shoes? What do you notice around you? Do you notice any sounds, sights, smells, or sensations on your skin or body? As you get to the mailbox, open it as slowly as possible. As you do, notice your shoulders, arms, and hands as you reach inside to grab the pieces of paper and mail waiting for you. Repeat that same slowness as you close the mailbox and return to your house. Feel your feet and body as you slowly walk back to where you were. You will likely need to remember what you are supposed to be doing in these two-minute exercises. You will get distracted. It is OK when you do; stop, slow down, and resume walking as slowly as possible. The goal is to be present and notice.

You can do this same exercise while eating. The next time you eat, try to make a game and see how slowly you can eat. Take two slow, mindful bites. As you do, notice your hand touching the utensil in your hand. Feel the connection in your arm as you raise your hand. See how slowly you can move. Feel the sensations around you as you place your spoon in your mouth. Feel the metal against your lips. As you take a bite, feel your mouth and tongue as you feel food inside your mouth. What sensations do you notice? What taste and textures do you notice? How does it make you feel? What does it smell like? Take a moment and savor what comes up for you and the delight you are experiencing. Mindful eating can transform your relationship with food. It encourages appreciation for the nourishment provided, aids digestion, and can help recognize true hunger and satiety signals.

Meditation is a form of mindfulness. The reason we want to practice mindfulness and meditation is so we can continue building our superpowers. So we can continue strengthening what is already deep inside of us. Mindfully take a bite of your food, as simple as it may sound. This act of noticing your food's taste, texture, and smell trains your brain. You are training yourself to notice to be more present. Being more present when it matters is critical, such as when you get upset or triggered or when someone needs your attention. Regularly practicing will enable you to be more present in these moments so you can be present rather than becoming hijacked or caught off guard by certain situations.

Mindfulness Examples:

Mindful Listening:

- Practice: Engage in a conversation where your sole focus is on truly listening to the other person. Notice the tone of their voice, their expressions, and the emotions behind their words. Refrain from planning your response while they speak. Instead, allow a brief pause after they've finished to fully absorb their message before you reply.

- Impact: This practice enhances your ability to be present with others, improving relationships and communication skills. It trains you to be less reactive and more thoughtful in interactions.

Nature Walks with Mindful Observation:

- Practice: Take a walk in a natural setting, whether at a park, a beach, or a trail. Make a conscious effort to observe your surroundings with all your senses. Notice the colors of the plants and sky, the texture of the ground under your feet, the sounds of wildlife, and the smell of the air. Each time your mind wanders to other thoughts, gently guide your attention back to these observations.

- Impact: This practice grounds you now, to the present moment, reducing stress and enhancing your connection with the outer world. It fosters a sense of peace and well-being by allowing you to step away from the busyness of daily life and immerse yourself in the simplicity and beauty of nature.

Integrating these mindfulness practices into your daily routine can significantly improve your awareness, reduce stress, and enhance your overall quality of life. They serve as simple yet powerful tools for cultivating a deeper sense of presence and connection in every moment.

Action Writing

One method is to practice writing to reinforce your value. I know affirmations and writing sound cheesy, right?! Trust me, the brain needs positive reinforcement.

Neuroscience of Writing:

Dr. David Rock created a study titled "The Neuroscience of Writing," which delves into the intricate relationship between writing, reflection, and neurological processes. His findings offer insights into how reflection writing can bolster leadership skills and decision-making capabilities. Through the lens of neuroscience, his studies reveal that writing and reflective thinking can solidify learning, deepen understanding, and aid in emotional regulation, enhancing leadership skills and decision-making capabilities. Many studies have been performed suggesting the benefits of writing. One study, in particular, at the University of Missouri shows that students who journaled five minutes a day, two to three days after a stressful or emotional event, were much more likely to accept the event and aid in emotional recovery, including quicker recovery time.

Accomplishment Writing:

Reflect on past successes, no matter how small, to solidify your belief in your capabilities. For example, I create an "accomplishment journal," or I tell my clients to create a journal and name it: "Why I'm a rockstar journal" or "Why I am a superhero journal" to document moments of achievement and growth. This practice nurtures self-appreciation and combats imposter syndrome. Get a notebook and allow yourself 45 minutes to sit and fully appreciate yourself. Think about every single accomplishment you have had. Did you graduate college? High School? Did you win a spelling bee? Did you learn how to ride a bike? Did you learn how to drive a manual car? Did you randomly pay for someone's coffee in a drive-thru? Did you learn a hobby or skill? Do you know multiple languages? Have you raised children? Did you take a shower today? (somedays, this is a huge accomplishment for me!). Your brain does not distinguish between small, medium, or large accomplishments. So write and write every single thing you can think of.

Now, sit with these accomplishments and feel them. Savor who you are. Savor what you have done. If you find yourself saying yes, but my cousin Sally's nephew is a nuclear physicist and is much more accomplished than me......**IMMEDIATE-LY say to yourself, STOP IT.**

Resume savoring who you are, what you have accomplished, and the feelings you are evoking and experiencing.

If you can, take five minutes to review your accomplishment journal and add to it every day. Each day, if you give yourself

3-5 accomplishments for the day, you will realize just how much of a rockstar superhero you are. You will begin to retrain yourself to default to feeling accomplished rather than feeling like an imposter.

EXERCISE: P.O.P.

The Power of the Pause allows you to move from an AU-TOPILOT reaction to being able to reset, find clarity, and then take action.

Stimuli >P.O.P.

Remember to create a physical anchor, such as snapping your fingers or slapping your hand on a table.

I snap my fingers and slap one of my legs to activate the P.O.P.

Stop. Breathe and allow the power of the pause to work for you.

By doing so, you are implementing your power to choose. The best part about P.O.P. is that it is so quick and easy!

It's disempowering to believe there is no freedom in action. ALL your freedom lies with the power of the pause because, in this time and space, you are allowing yourself to calm your emotions, avoiding a knee-jerk reaction, and choosing a wise and appropriately powerful response for you.

> **People don't control your emotions; they only activate them.**

As a young child and young adult, most of the emotional influences I witnessed were a see-saw of complete disinterest/apathy or complete rage. My method and model for expressing emotion was pure rage. Because I learned this was my default emotion, I had to teach myself the power of the pause to discern my emotions from others and ask myself what was most important to me when dealing with others.

The power lies in ownership. Take ownership of your emotions rather than give that power away. When working with teams, spotting those with low emotional intelligence is easy because one might easily blame others rather than take ownership and explore how others feel.

The more you practice the P.O.P. to give yourself space to make a more empowering decision, the more you train your brain to pause and connect your emotions to your power. This practice creates new neural pathways to default to robust, more automatic responses rather than knee-jerk, hasty, angry responses.

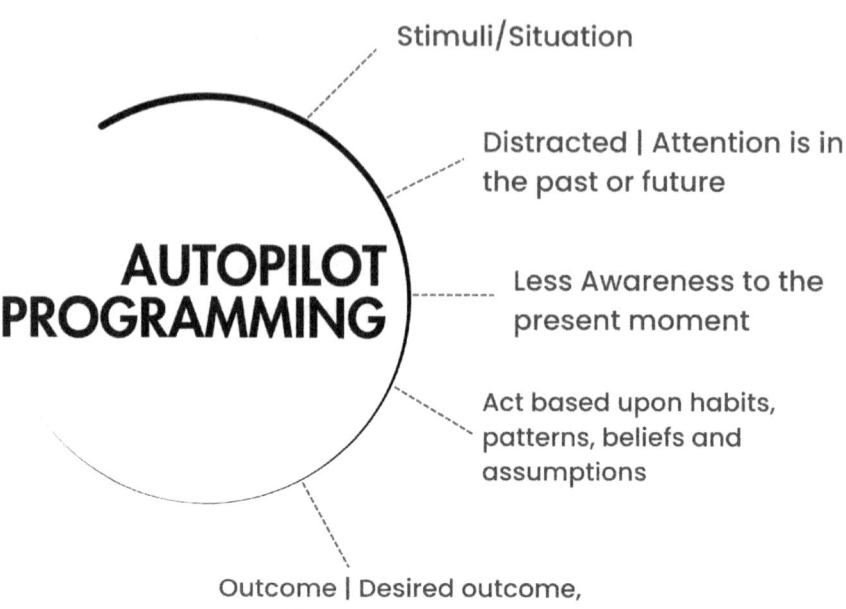

Stimuli/Situation

Distracted | Attention is in the past or future

AUTOPILOT PROGRAMMING

Less Awareness to the present moment

Act based upon habits, patterns, beliefs and assumptions

Outcome | Desired outcome, or not?

EMOTION TRUTH DETECTOR

The "Emotion Truth Detector" exercise is a tool I designed to enhance emotional intelligence by helping you identify, understand, and articulate your emotions accurately. This exercise encourages introspection and self-awareness, enabling you to navigate your emotional landscape and the emotions of those around you more effectively.

For example, a leader might use this tool during a conflict situation to discern their emotional state and the underlying feelings of team members, leading to a more empathetic and constructive resolution. By practicing this exercise, leaders can develop a keener sense of emotional awareness, improving their ability to communicate, manage stress, and make decisions that consider the emotional dynamics of their teams.

The idea behind the emotion truth detector is for you to answer the question: is the emotion a truth or a lie? Because our automatic responses to ourselves and our emotions are often self-deprecating or harmful based upon old patterns and false beliefs, we must stop the pattern and determine if the emotion is a truth or a lie. Then, create a new story to develop a new pattern.

THE EMOTION TRUTH DETECTOR EXERCISE:

- Stop...Breath...Notice what comes up...

- What is the situation?

- Notice the emotion...(I feel kind of crappy...I feel kind of sad, or frustrated...or angry...)

- Ask yourself: is this a lie/or truth?...

- What is the lie? (What is the lie that God/Spirit/Universe Refuses to believe?)

- What is the truth? (What is the truth that God/Spirit/Universe believes to be true)

- Then ask yourself...are you CHOOSING to place your thoughts to lead to an emotion that is NOT TRUE?

- Now shifting into a different frequency of attitude based upon the TRUTH...(rather than the lie)...feel the truth...

- How does this feel?

- Awareness is a crucial step. When you are aware of your emotion(s) you can name them and then work through how to view them.

- Then take a step back to notice what comes up, what is the feeling, what is the experience?

"**Anybody can become angry-that is easy, but to be angry with the right person, and to the right degree, and at the right time, and for the right purpose, and in the right way that is not within everybody's power and is not easy.**" **Aristotle**

Example:

My boss didn't recognize my effort on a project and ignored me...I felt discouraged and sad.

I immediately feel I am stupid and unimportant.

The lie behind this feeling is that I feel like I'm stupid and unimportant.

The truth behind this lie is that I am very important and quite intelligent. I feel good when I know I am important and cared for.

I choose to feel important and am a capable, intelligent being.

I choose not to believe my lie and believe the truth.

The Emotion Truth Detector PRACTICE:

Stop...Breath...Notice what comes up...

What is the situation?

Notice the emotion...(I feel kind of crappy...I feel kind of sad, or frustrated...or angry...)

Ask yourself: is this a lie/or truth?...

What is the lie? (What is the lie that God/Spirit/Universe Refuses to believe?)

What is the truth? (What is the truth that God/Spirit/Universe believes to be true)

Then ask yourself...are you CHOOSING to place your thoughts to lead to an emotion that is NOT TRUE?

Now shifting into a different frequency of attitude based upon the TRUTH...(rather than the lie)...feel the truth...How does this feel?

THE COST OF BELIEF

What are your beliefs costing you? What are your disbeliefs costing you?

10 Step Belief Buster Formula

Similar to the emotion truth detector, below is a formula you can use to rewrite a belief and uncover the truth to create a new belief and a more empowered perspective for yourself.

Belief: Now, think about a belief.

i.e., Money isn't easy to come by. Only some people become happy and rich and successful. Money doesn't grow on trees.

What causes this belief? What story did you hear about, or maybe what is the meaning behind the belief? Why/Where did this come from?

i.e., I witnessed everyone around me struggle, and my parents would say these things to me.

What is your secondary gain by having these beliefs? (there is ALWAYS a secondary gain. Why am I holding on to this belief?

i.e., It keeps me safe. It keeps me comfortable. To feel or think differently would mean I would have to be different. It's easier for me to blame someone else.

Holding on to this belief is costing me?

i.e., loss of time, loss of productivity, loss of relationships, loss of connecting with kids and others, costing me my health, to gain weight, to be unhealthy, to be exhausted, to be worn down, loss of income, loss of growth, loss of marriage)

Subset of this question: One year from now...what will all of the above cost me.... ie. Regret and pain...

Poke holes: Is this true for everyone? Has there ever been a time in your life when this belief was NOT true?

i.e., There are people who make money effortlessly. I have witnessed many people who are money magnets. I get random gifts, random checks, new clients, windfalls,

Let Go: What is the NEW TRUTH TO THIS NEW STO-RY?

i.e., Money is easy to make, and People with it are generous and kind and make an impact.

If you operate from this NEW TRUTH PERSPECTIVE ...What types of change would occur?

i.e., Abundance, more money, more freedom, more connection, and quality, because of generosity and impact

DECLARATION TIME....Do you choose a new version of this story OR do you choose to remain in the old version of this story? Assuming you're choosing new! What is a statement you declare right now:

i.e., Abundance and Making Money is Easy to Make and Keep. It comes to me effortlessly in divine order in perfect ways.

TALK IS CHEAP!

What is one ACTION you will take RIGHT NOW as you believe this new statement? What will prove that your action supports your new belief?

i.e., Calling someone. Asking for a new client or a new contact, paying a bill, buying something, gifting, donating, randomly giving someone money...

SAVOR the feelings of gratitude for the lessons the belief has taught you...now savor the feelings of achievement and what it is like living the new truth...

Gratitude Toolbox

Inspired by "The Neurological Magic of Gratitude"

Daily Gratitude Journaling:

Amplify happiness and life satisfaction by writing down three new things you're grateful for daily. This practice enhances personal well-being and potentially enriches those around us.

Gratitude Letters:

Once a month, write and send (or deliver in person) a letter of gratitude to someone who has significantly impacted your life.

This exercise is backed by findings that suggest such acts of gratitude can increase happiness levels for both the sender and recipient, catalyzing a positive feedback loop in relationships.

Dopamine-Boosting Gratitude Meditation:

Engage in daily meditation focused on gratitude to stimulate dopamine production, the neurochemical linked with pleasure and reward.

This practice can rewire the brain towards more positive and grateful thought patterns, enhancing overall well-being.

Expressive Gratitude in Relationships:

Make it a habit to verbally express gratitude to at least one person daily, whether personally or professionally.

This act of bridge-building fosters deeper connections and amplifies mutual appreciation and positivity.

Workplace Gratitude Practices:

Implement simple yet meaningful gestures of appreciation within your team or organization, such as publicly acknowledging team members' contributions or sharing gratitude moments in meetings.

These practices can elevate morale, increase productivity, and improve employee retention.

Gratitude Reflections and Exercises:

Incorporate reflection prompts and practical exercises into your routine. Reflect on the last time you expressed gratitude, think of someone you haven't thanked recently, and find gratitude in challenging moments.

Gratitude Walks:

Regularly engage in gratitude walks, where with each step, you think of something you're grateful for.

This practice combines the benefits of physical activity with mindfulness, enhancing both physical and mental health.

Setting Daily Gratitude Reminders:

Use an app or a calendar reminder to your advantage by setting daily reminders to pause and reflect on something you're grateful for.

This can serve as a powerful tool to reset and refocus during busy or stressful days.

Gratitude as a Leadership Tool:

Leaders can model gratitude by starting meetings with a round of appreciation or establishing a culture where gratitude is openly expressed and shared.

This approach strengthens team bonds and sets a positive tone for collaborative efforts.

Chapter Summary:

By integrating these tools into daily life, we can harness the neurological magic of gratitude to transform not only our brains and emotional states but also our relationships and business cultures. Gratitude is not just a feeling but a powerful catalyst for positive change, capable of enhancing our lives in profound ways.

By leaning into calm, making decisions with a clear mind, and acting courageously, you're not just reacting; you're proactively engaging with your inner strengths. This approach requires not just understanding but also embodying the principles of emotional intelligence and resilience.

Each time you successfully navigate a challenging situation by employing your toolkit, you're not merely overcoming a hurdle but reinforcing your superpowers, building them up to be stronger and more reliable.

This journey of building superpowers is similar to training any muscle; it requires dedication, repetition, and a willingness to push through discomfort. The tools in your personal toolkit—whether they involve mindfulness practices, cognitive reframing, or physiological techniques to calm the nervous system—are your exercises. Regularly applying these tools, especially in moments of calm, prepares you for the moments of storm.

As you develop these superpowers, you'll find that you recover more quickly from emotional hijacks and begin to navigate life with a more profound sense of confidence, resilience, and emotional agility.

Empowerment through action is not just about achieving goals but about the journey—how we face challenges, honor our commitments, and grow through our experiences. By embracing this path with integrity, awareness, and a willingness to learn from every situation, we achieve our aspirations and become the best versions of ourselves.

Chapter Nine

It Feels Good to Be Alive

"I believe in believe" ~ Ted Lasso

On a frigid February night, I found myself awake, wrestling with the gravity of the decision I placed in front of myself. Is this really what I wanted to do? Thoughts raced through my head as I struggled to seek the answer. Seventeen at the time, I sat up all night in my bed with a pen and notebook on my lap; I wrote all the reasons I could think of that were on my mind. My pain and struggle were the core of my motivations, caught in a lifelong battle of anxiety and depression with overwhelming feelings that I do not matter. The voice in my head nagged at me, yelling. "You're worthless" and "You would be better off dead." These common phrases of inner voice overshadowed any reason my cognitive mind could override.

Seeking a beacon of support, I approached my mother weeks earlier, yearning for validation and understanding. Nervous but sheepishly, I said, "Mom, I have been thinking about killing myself." Her silence at the time was devastating, as she replied with a blank face and no words, only to return to me days later with a bone-chilling almost angry reply "Heather, what you told me really hurt me, I wish you had not told me this."

Wow, my own mother confirmed what I already felt: Unseen, unheard, and unimportant. At that moment, all my hope circuits quickly drained from my soul.

The cold February night was quickly fading into the morning. Knowing my father would be getting up soon to take me to school, I had to act quickly. As dawn approached, I reached the point of no return, resolved in my decision. My mind was made up; my life was over. I went into the kitchen cabinets, collected every pill bottle I could, grabbed a giant glass of water, and returned to bed. Handful by handful, I swallowed the pills in hopes the pain I felt would finally end. Then, with a sense of relief, I lay down to go to sleep, hoping not to wake up.

Soon after, my father found me in my bed, frantic and overwhelmed with disbelief at what I had just done. In a whirlwind of urgency, my father rushed me to the hospital. He quickly found a close family friend who worked there and navigated me through the hospital's flurry, orchestrating a rapid response to save my life. So much of that early morning was a blur to me as I was in and out of consciousness with scenes and memories of my life coming in and out of my mind.

My grandparents arrived, and I will never forget the look on their faces as they were in complete shock and horror with no idea I felt the way I did, as I had concealed my true feelings from them. I heard whispers from the nurses and doctors, wondering why and how a 17-year-old girl could do such a thing.

Eventually, when I was stable enough to be conscious enough to communicate with the doctors. As I was lying on an uncomfortable, stark hospital bed in the cold emergency room, one doctor, as he was checking on me, asked why I would do such a thing. I shrugged my shoulders and sheepishly said, "Stuff".

He replied back, "This wasn't over a boy, was it?" Life immediately returned to my face as my blood rushed into my veins, partially over the embarrassment that this was what the doctor thought my reason was for wanting to take my own life. To which I immediately replied in a stern, firm, and emphatic voice, "My goodness, NO, I may be suicidal, but I'm not crazy." The doctor had a good laugh out loud and came to me, put his hand on my shoulder, looked at me square in the eye, and said, "I am now confident you are going to be okay." And luckily, I was.

Over the next six weeks, I attended an in-patient counseling center and went through some pretty intensive therapy. And it was terrific. For the first time in my life, I felt I had a voice. I felt I mattered. And I learned how to start understanding how to view and process my feelings and emotions. One of the significant discoveries I learned was how I had used my 'rose-colored glasses' for survival in my childhood to help protect and shield me from the trauma and unpleasant experiences I faced.

I also learned to be honest about who my parents were, their challenges, and how I fit into a world that was not perfect as I had created in my mind. I had been self-advocating and taking care of myself most of my life, and I felt that if I admitted to the world that my life and my family were not perfect, the world would somehow not accept me.

Through the healing process, I learned how to look inward for self-discovery. I learned that my superpower was accepting myself and loving myself, flaws and all. Even though I followed through with one of the most traumatic experiences and awful ways to cry for help, this experience ironically saved my life.

I never wanted to die. I just wanted to feel differently. I wanted to live but didn't know how else to ask for help.

I missed a significant amount of school during my recovery period. However, I was focused and more present than ever, learning to live life in a new way with newfound hope and excitement. I was keeping up with my school work and growing and learning for the first time ever. At the same time, I was learning coping and emotional management skills.

One day, I was sitting in my principal's office, trying to explain my intentions on my recovery, the support I needed, and how I wanted to finish my schooling. He informed me that he and my doctors discussed what they felt was best for me.

"Wait a second. Do you mean you and my doctors have been having conversations about my future? And what is best for me? And without me or my parents involved?" I questioned him in shock.

He replied, "Yes, and we feel you're just embarrassed, and it would be best if you just returned to school as normal."

Fury ignited within me—not at the possibility they might be right, but at the audacity of their unilateral decision about my future.

It was apparent they knew my parents were not advocating for me, so they did not even bother to talk with my parents or me.

And once again, I felt as if I didn't matter, as if I did not have a voice. At that moment, I was angry. I was hurt. And I decided to take my power back.

My anger caused me to P.O.P.

This P.O.P., however, was a healthy anger because it gave me a moment to take control of what was important to me.

So I practiced what I didn't realize then was a very powerful tool, the power of the pause, and POPPED.

I just stopped and gave myself time to feel what I felt best and how I wanted to respond.

The moment of clarity hit me—the moment of power. And I took control of my power and understood who I was and wanted to be. I needed to be in control of my emotions rather than letting anyone or any circumstance be in control, and I felt it.

So I did. I said, "No." "No. I will not be returning to school. Either you let me finish on my terms through the recovery, as I am doing now, or I quit."

He said, "Well, your only option is to return to school; this is what we've already decided."

So I said, "Okay then, I quit." And I stood up and started to walk out of his office.

The irony of this situation was he did not even get my name right. As I was walking away and getting ready to leave his office, the man who felt he knew what was best for me, the one making decisions with other adults about my life, said to me, "Thank you, Heidi."

I immediately turn around and say, "Excuse me, what's my name?" He stuttered and stammered, confused, as if I had insulted him. I repeated myself and said, "What did you call me? Tell me my name?" And he froze, staring at me.

With newfound resolve, I corrected him, "My name is Heather. Remember it." Marking a pivotal assertion of my identity as I walked out of his office, never to return again.

In that moment, for the first time in my life, I had never stood so powerful and strong. He was in shock, and his mouth was agape.

Still angry but feeling liberated, I immediately called my physician's office and said to him, "This is my life, and because you don't care enough to understand or believe in me, it's time for me to believe in myself. I want you to know that I just quit school."

So I did. I quit school at the end of my junior year, not because I wanted to quit but because I wanted to believe in myself and take my power back.

From the ashes of that tumultuous period, how did I rise to become a college graduate, a business owner, a CEO, and a high-performance neuro coach? The answer is simple: I chose me. I chose to believe in me.

"Belief doesn't just happen cause you hang something on the wall. It comes from the heart, up in the brain, and down in the gut." Ted Lasso

The day I quit high school, I immediately went to the local adult services organization and quickly went through the process to get my GED. The reason was so I could go to college. And that's precisely what I did. I was finishing my first year of college when my high school class was finishing high school! I needed to move away and stand in my power. It was time for me to believe in myself.

For the first 17 years of my life, I remained relatively silent, enveloped in a cloak of guardedness and shyness. My instinct was to blend into the background, a survival mechanism to shield me from harm and maintain a semblance of safety. This tendency and the dynamics I witnessed growing up instilled a profound sense of insignificance in me. However, the realization that I possessed a voice—a voice that could articulate my thoughts and desires—marked a pivotal transformation in my self-perception. It dawned on me that I indeed mattered, igniting a profound shift within.

No longer would I resign myself to the shadows; I refused to be silenced or rendered invisible any longer. In this awakening, I discovered my inner strength and superpower: a steadfast belief in my worth. This epiphany propelled me to advocate for myself, to assert my presence, and to claim my space in the world with conviction.

Iron Man said, "To make an omelet, sometimes you must break some eggs." I broke some eggs, alright, but not out of defiance or rebelliousness but out of power and desire to create a bigger vision for myself. I had to step up. Then, I need to find the right people to help me. Understanding my values helped me seek a bigger vision for myself, one that I created because of my belief in myself rather than a vision that had been given to me. This is the underlying lesson of all. My values and my vision have been my guiding principles ever since.

Since then, my path has been strewn with obstacles, requiring me to rebuild my understanding of myself and the world around me. I've learned that our beliefs, often rooted in negativity for survival's sake, can anchor us to our limitations or propel us toward our fullest potential. These beliefs shape our capacity for love, trust, and taking risks. However, the realization that I could reshape these beliefs was liberating. I transformed from being shrouded in shame for my origins to embracing every experience as a part of my perfectly imperfect self. I discovered that hoarding my stories, clinging to an image of who I thought I should be, was a disservice to my authentic self and to those seeking a similar retreat.

Embarking on this journey, I chose to redefine my identity, viewing the world through a new lens of possibilities crafted by my own aspirations. This was not merely about seeing the world differently but fundamentally altering my interaction with it, transforming challenges into canvases for my desires.

This transformation taught me an invaluable lesson about our interconnectedness. Each of us carries a unique tapestry of experience, yet we share the common thread of the human condition. Whether engaging with a client, aiding a team's growth, or sharing a moment with a stranger, we navigate a world rich with stories and scars. Acknowledging and sharing these parts of ourselves can transform our interactions, moving from isolation to a sense of collective harmony.

Expanding on this, engaging with others in a meaningful way requires us to see beyond the superficial to recognize and honor the vast spectrum of human experiences. It's about understanding that our stories, filled with their own triumphs and trials, resonate with universal themes of struggle, resilience, and the quest for belonging. By embracing our own narratives and valuing those of others, we cultivate a deeper sense of connection and empathy. This doesn't just enrich our personal lives; it transforms our communities, creating spaces where everyone feels seen, heard, and valued.

The act of changing our perceptions opens up a world overflowing with potential. It invites us to view life not as a sequence of hurdles but as a realm of endless opportunity. Each experience, each interaction, becomes a chance to grow, learn, and connect on a profound level. This is how we turn life's challenges into stepping stones towards a more prosperous, fulfilling existence.

Imagine riding your bicycle through a universe that, at first glance, appears only in shades of black and white—where everything feels somewhat heavy and dark, possibly offering a false sense of security because of its predictability. In this monochromatic world, you're perpetually on edge, anticipating challenges at every turn, your path defined by fear and doubt. Then you dig deep, use your tools in your toolbox to help you tap into your superpowers where you remember all that is possible. As you cross the threshold into a world awash in Technicolor, everything transforms, **beginning to shimmer**. Suddenly, you become surrounded by opportunities, joy, fulfillment, peace, calm, connection, love—everything you've ever desired. Most crucially, you carry with you the unshakable belief that no matter where your journey takes you, you possess the tools and resources to experience life's depth fully, a belief without limits that empowers you and others. Imagine inspiring those around you to see their existence in this radiant Technicolor, sparking a wave of empowerment, positivity, and boundless potential. Herein lies our true superpower: to empower ourselves and inspire others to perceive their world in vivid color as well.

I feel an immense sense of gratitude and happiness for being alive and well. I am confident in my abilities, and I credit my grandmother for instilling this belief in me. Equipped with the necessary tools and superpowers from my toolbox, I embrace every moment of my life in full Technicolor. My hope is that you too can live your life to the fullest.

Chapter Ten

Conclusion

"It's about who you are, accepting yourself. Until you do, happiness will be a stranger." ~ Unknown

Believe In Yourself More Than Your Grandma: Unleash your Superpower Through Simple Neuroscience

This journey transcends mere stress management, marking a profound exploration into self-discovery and neural adaptation. It encourages embracing practices that foster awareness and establishing core habits that align with our deepest values. This path addresses the challenges of our instinctive reactions and reshapes our perception of the world, leveraging our brain's potential to mold our experiences and life outcomes. We embark on a transformative journey by understanding the neuroscience behind our emotions and employing mindfulness. It's a process of learning to navigate our inner landscapes with grace, aiming for a state of fulfillment and emotional intelligence guided by the principles of vulnerability and self-compassion. This approach promises a more authentic, interconnected existence, turning our emotions from barriers into gateways for profound self-understanding and connection with the world.

TAKING BELIEF INTO ORGANIZATIONS:

Research consistently shows that belief, both in oneself and in one's leaders, plays a crucial role in the success and well-being of employees and the overall productivity of the workplace. Thriving employees who are deeply engaged and report high well-being overwhelmingly tend to be those who have a strong belief in their abilities to perform their roles effectively. These individuals not only achieve higher job satisfaction and performance but also experience lower stress levels. Similarly, leaders with a robust belief in their leadership capabilities significantly enhance team dynamics, fostering an environment that supports positivity, collaboration, and high performance.

Moreover, leaders who strongly believe in their visions and capabilities inspire greater organizational commitment, engagement, and effort among their team members. This leadership style, centered on self-belief, belief, and confidence, is increasingly recognized as vital in today's work culture, emphasizing the creation of empowering and growth-focused environments for employees.

These insights underscore a simple yet profound truth: the foundation of a thriving, productive work environment is built on the mutual self-belief of employees and leaders alike. This shared confidence fosters deeper trust, a sense of belonging, and a secure and positive workplace atmosphere where people are motivated to excel, innovate, and face challenges with resilience. Ultimately, a culture of self-belief not only elevates individual and team performance but also cultivates a workplace where everyone can strive for excellence and extraordinary achievements with less stress and more fulfillment.

BELIEF JOURNEY

Reflecting on the journey this book takes you through, from the depths of self-discovery to the heights of neural rewiring, we've navigated the intricate dance between belief, action, and transformation. As we close this chapter, consider it not the end but a vibrant beginning to a life lived in Technicolor—a life where belief is not just a concept but your unwavering superpower.

Through the stories and neuroscience explored within these pages, we've seen how our perceptions, deeply ingrained in our neural pathways, shape our reality. The tales of overcoming, from personal battles to professional triumphs, illustrate the potent force of belief. In the workplace, this belief fosters environments where creativity, productivity, and well-being flourish, underscoring the transformative power of a collective conviction in our abilities and visions.

This book is a call to action: to embrace your superpower of belief, to paint your world with the colors of possibility and joy. Let it be a reminder that every moment is an opportunity to rewrite your story, to change the lens through which you view the world, and to step into a future where you are the creator of your destiny.

So, as you step forth from this reading journey, carry with you the knowledge that belief in yourself, in your capabilities, and in the possibilities that life offers, is the cornerstone of living with purpose, passion, and empowerment. Let this belief be the light that guides you through the challenges, the beacon that illuminates your path to success, and the force that propels you to live each day to its fullest potential.

Remember, the mind is everything. What you think, you become. Use belief as your superpower, and take back your power. As you move forward, let the vibrant hues of Technicolor guide your way, illuminating a path filled with hope, resilience, and the joy of a life well-lived. Let's inspire a world where belief is not just a word but the essence of our being, driving us toward a future of boundless possibilities and profound empowerment.

It's Your Power. Take It Back.

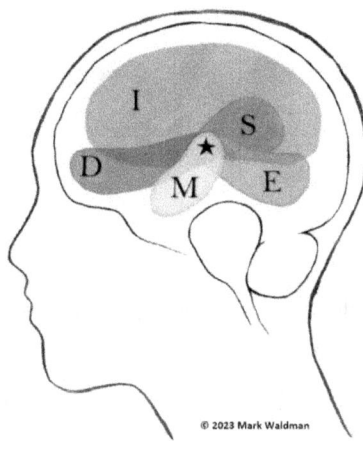

© 2023 Mark Waldman

The "DIMES" in Your Brain

Key brain networks influenced by the "Relaxed Mindful Awareness" strategies of NeuroCoaching

D   **Doing / Attention:** Executive Networks

I   **Imagination:** Default Network

M   **Motivation** Network

E   **Emotional** Networks

S   **Value / Social Awareness:** Salience Network

✱   Learning/Awareness: (Insula, anterior cingulate, hippocampus, amygdala)

Panksepp's Core Emotions:
SEEKING / Curiosity
PLAY / Social Joy
CARE
GRIEF
FEAR
RAGE
LUST

What's Next

Please take a moment and send back your comments and feedback. Your input is invaluable to us!

Want rapid development for rapid results?

Our mission is to superpower your people so you can superpower your brand and business.

Learn more about our tools to help you reach your goals faster, smarter, and cheaper and unleash your superpowers!

Contact hello@heatherjcrider.com

Visit for more information

www.HeatherJCrider.com

www.RockstarPerformanceAcademy.com

Acknowledgements

This book's catalyst and inspiration came from my grand-mother, Joyce Payne, a.k.a Gemma. The self-belief I've learned, borrowed, faked, and created, all started with the unwavering steadfast belief she held for me since I was born. Thank you, Gemma. Your spirit and presence have been with me daily since you left this earth. Your legacy lives on, and I am eternally grateful to you.

To my children, Audrey and Sawyer. Thank you for allow-ing me to grow as a person, to try new things and fail, to exper-iment with life and succeed. Thank you for letting me process my emotions, sometimes with grace, sometimes without grace. Thank you for letting me learn how to be honest with you about how I feel. Thank you for allowing me to learn who I am and for me to be me. Thank you for being my greatest teachers and biggest joys. I love you both so much.

From the moment I met my incredible partner, Mark Schul-man, my life has been immeasurably uplifted, enriched, and transformed. Thank you for being a reservoir of inspiration, wisdom, hope, excitement, and support. Your unwavering belief in me has ignited renewed self-confidence and belief within. Your spirit, love, and drive enchant me daily, and I am deeply thankful for your presence and love in my life.

To my Uncle, Winston Churchhill Crider—your relentless belief in me, your unwavering support, candid advice, and boundless love have guided me in more ways than words can express. Thank you.

Thank you to my sister, parents, grandparents, and entire extended family. Though our journey together has been tumultuous at times, the experiences and lessons I've gained from you have shaped the person I am today. I am deeply grateful.

Thank you to my mentors, teachers, and guides who have taught me how to borrow and rekindle belief in moments of doubt, despair, and confusion. A special thanks to John Barada, aka JJB3, and Tessa Greenspan—my surrogate parents!

I want to express my gratitude to Mark Waldman and the entire NeuroWisdom and NeuroCoach Pro team. Your inspiration and guidance inspired my passion for neuroscience and my desire to study it. You have positively impacted my life and empowered me to share my beliefs with others.

My friends, fans, and supporters, you have inspired me to be brave enough to write this book. Also, specifically, thank you to Amy Williamson, who has been a constant encourager and cheerleader. You're awesome, Amy.

Thank you to all the individuals from whom I have had the privilege to learn, those I have coached, and those who have inspired me from afar. Your guidance, wisdom, and inspiration have been the foundation of my growth, bestowing me invaluable lessons and opportunities that have profoundly shaped who I am today and the self-belief I now hold.

To Ted Lasso for believing in "believe." Although a fictional character, this is invaluable wisdom.

About the author

Heather J. Crider is a Certified Neuroperformance Coach who empowers overwhelmed professionals to unleash brain-powered breakthroughs, unlock paramount performance, create unrelenting energy, and build deeper human connections.

Heather is a master at Unleashing Superpowers. She focuses on elevating companies, leaders, and people through neuroperformance experiences, discovering untapped strengths for cohesive collaboration and collective excellence.

Grounded and mentored in the most advanced research from the most recognized thought leaders in neuroscience at the world's top institutions (Harvard, Princeton, Yale, MIT, Wharton, Brown, etc.) Heather J. Crider is one of our nation's few certified coaches in both neuroscience and the emerging fields of neuro-performance and neuro-leadership.

With a discerning bias toward a practical, evidence-based approach, industry-leading companies worldwide tap Heather's uniquely honed, highly engaging, neuroscience-based ability to empower overwhelmed professionals to beat burnout, equip leaders with exceptional resilience, unleash brain-powered breakthroughs, deepen human connections, and unlock both boundless energy and superlative performance.

On behalf of her global clients, Heather is currently pioneering new research and methodology, using the uniquely potent interface of music and neuroscience to achieve optimal (measurable) gains in engagement, performance, and results.

As Co-Creator of The Everyday Rockstar Performance Leadership Academy, Heather and her global research team have developed a distinctively interactive, AI-enabled, and practical brain-based approach that measurably reduces stress while enhancing emotional intelligence, performance, and focus at individual, group, and organizational levels.

Heather has been a sought-after keynote speaker and thought leader at conferences and associations for over 15 years and hosts the Go Reflect Yourself Podcast. As a neuroscience coach and neuro-practice pioneer, Heather has appeared on numerous podcasts and webinars and has been featured in Forbes, Yahoo Finance, Brainz Magazine, and Thrive Global.

To book Heather to speak at your conference or event, contact hello@heatherjcrider.com

Do you have a favorite tequila, coffee bean, or neuroscience tip to share?

(no, those three things are not related at all)...These are just some of Heather's favorites. She loves exploring and learning about new tequila, coffee, and anything brain-based!

Please email hello@heatherjcrider.com

www.heatherjcrider.com

Believe in Yourself More Than Your Grandma
By Heather Crider

Are you ready to unlock the true potential that's been hiding within you? **Believe in Yourself More Than Your Grandma** offers a game-changing approach for ambitious professionals and entrepreneurs who are tired of self-doubt holding them back. Author Heather Crider merges practical neuroscience with transformative strategies to help you tap into your brain's innate abilities, empowering you to create high-performance teams and achieve extraordinary results.

What You'll Discover in This Book:

- The science behind self-belief and how to **reprogram your brain for success**

- How to harness your brain's **superpower** to overcome self-doubt and achieve peak performance

- **Actionable strategies** for building empowered, high-performing teams

- Real-life examples and insights to guide you on your journey to **leadership excellence**

- A unique fusion of personal empowerment, neuroscience, and practical tools that you can apply immediately

Who Is This Book For?

- Entrepreneurs and business leaders looking to elevate their teams and themselves

- Professionals who want to crush self-doubt and step into their full potential

- Anyone who's ready to use neuroscience-backed techniques to **master their mindset** and achieve unstoppable success

Through engaging stories, solid scientific backing, and Heather's powerful insights, this book is more than just self-help—it's a roadmap to becoming the best version of yourself. Whether you're tackling leadership challenges or striving for personal growth, **Believe in Yourself More Than Your Grandma** gives you the tools to **turn aspirations into achievements**.